Breakfast in Palestine

Learning Culture Through Family and Food

Dixiane Hallaj

S & H Publishing, Inc.
Purcellville, Virginia USA

S & H Publishing, Inc.
P. O. Box 456
Purcellville, VA 20134
www.sandhbooks.com

Ordering Information:
Quantity discounts are available. For details, contact the "Special Sales Department" at the address above or email sales@sandhpublishing.com.

Title/Dixiane Hallaj
Memoir, Middle East, Palestine, Jordan, War, Travel, Creative Nonfiction
ISBN 978-1-63320-077-7 Print Edition
ISBN 978-1-63320-078-4 Ebook Edition

Table of Contents

Palestine?

LATE SPRING 1962. My father sat across from me in a small restaurant, enjoying his food and half listening to me babble about university life and the boy I was dating.

"What?" he exclaimed, suddenly catching up to my words. "Vermont? The capital of Georgia?" The restaurant went quiet.

Dad and I stared at each other for a few seconds, then we both started laughing uncontrollably. Around us, the clank of cutlery and murmur of conversations resumed.

"Amman, the capital of Jordan," I said as soon as I could speak. "Actually, he's from Palestine."

"Palestine? Like in the Bible?"

* * *

Everyone's heard of the Philistines, right? Well, Filistine is Arabic for Palestine. The Philistines and the Canaanites, both tribes of ancient Palestine, had cultures that were well developed and flourishing when Moses led his people out of Egypt.

We all know that history is written by the victors, and the word Philistine has come to symbolize someone who is hostile, or at best indifferent, to culture and the arts. However, examples of early Philistine art have survived to this day in the form of statuary and ceramic vessels and figurines. But art is not limited to the fine arts.

One of the oldest artistic traditions in Palestine is weaving textiles. Fine linen textiles have been discovered and dated to the 4th millennia BC. To this day, Palestine

1

has an ongoing rich culture of all types of art, including textile art, that reaches every segment of the population.

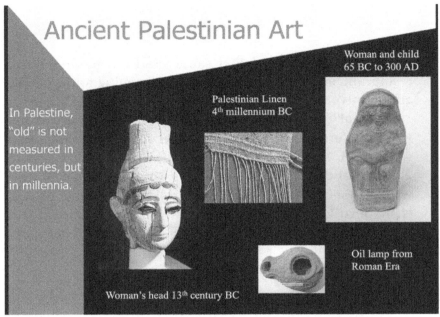

From a presentation to the Loudoun County Fine Arts Association

Poetry and music also have a history in Palestine that reaches far beyond the boundaries of recorded history. Poets are recognized and revered, singers are often immortalized, and everyone dances at weddings and other celebrations.

But the ever-present part of the culture that is passed from generation to generation and so much a part of life that it is like the air we breathe is the food we eat. Food is literally a part of us. We *are* the food we eat.

Just as the water in a fishbowl is invisible to the fish, the common foods can be unseen and unnoticed by the people who take them for granted. Eclipsed by a few signature dishes of a region, the common foods and the traditions surrounding them are a part of culture, too.

When I married a Palestinian, I began the slow process of learning how to exist in a cross-cultural world, but it wasn't until I moved with my husband and two small children to live as part of his family during very trying and stressful times that I began to appreciate what a gift I had received.

* * *

During our fifty-five-year marriage, the perception of Palestine and Palestinians changed. Fueled by the continued expansion of Israel's borders, and an increasingly desperate population, the Palestinians have tried by all means available to make their voices heard.

My hope is that this book will open a window into the Palestinian culture and community that I have loved for nearly three-quarters of a century.

The Beginning

"May I join you?" I heard a man's voice behind me. My lunch companion's bushy mustache stretched over his grin, confirming that he was the one being asked.

"Sure, have a seat." A cup of coffee clinked onto the table and chair legs scraped along the well-worn floor tiles of the student union.

The introductions were a blur as I fell into the deepest pair of liquid brown eyes I'd ever seen. The two men sparred with the easy banter of good friends, and the words ping-ponged around me. It took a few minutes for the conversation to penetrate the fog of Wow. I flicked my long straight hair out of the way and held up my hands.

"Stop. Wait a minute. Did you just ask how his war was going? In Algeria?" It was early 1962, and even I was aware of the seven-year Algerian war of independence. I ran to classes in shorts and bare feet, read Jack Kerouac, listened to folk music, and sang about freedom. The Civil Rights Movement had made the songs mainstream popular, but I, along with many of my friends, was trying to take a broader view of freedom. Not just here, everywhere.

"Yup. That's him. Muhammad Hallaj, the University of Florida's guerrilla fighter." I smiled, not following the thought enough to join in the laughter. I'd heard about gorilla fighters in the news. It didn't make a lot of sense. Why were they called gorilla fighters since they were fighting in cities rather than jungles?

Trying not to look too deeply into the brown eyes and lose myself again, I asked, "Didn't you say you were from Jordan? Algeria's way over in the west of North Africa." I

4

waved my left hand. "But Jordan's in the fertile crescent, isn't it?" I waved my right hand and winced as the words left my mouth. How lame was that? I must look like a sea bird sitting on the pier with wings outstretched to the sun. I lowered my arms and hid my hands in my lap.

"I'm actually Palestinian, but we're all Arabs." The brown eyes turned their full intensity on me, and butterflies fluttered in my insides. I hoped I wasn't blushing.

It wasn't until the second cup of coffee that I got up the courage to ask, "If you're from Jordan, why do you say you are Palestinian?"

"You have the question backward. If I'm Palestinian, why am I carrying a Jordanian passport?"

"Okay, consider the question flipped."

"Do you know that the United Nations created the state of Israel?"

"Yes. I actually just read a book about it." Just before I blurted out that the book was *Exodus* by Leon Uris and how much I'd enjoyed it, the penny dropped. He was probably one of the people on the "other" side.

A smothered chuckle reminded me why I was there in the first place.

"Do you still want the notes from Friday's class, Bill?"

"Oh, no. I can't leave now. This is too much fun."

Even if I didn't say the name, they both knew which book I meant because it had been on the *New York Times* best seller list for months and was still going strong.

Muhammad explained with a summary he must have repeated countless times, but his words held meaning and real emotion. "To make a long story short, the land that the UN gave to Israel wasn't theirs to give. And when Israel was through grabbing everything it could, we were left with about twenty per cent of our country, so the UN generously gave that to Jordan. That made me and nearly two million other Palestinians citizens of Jordan."

He tried to say it lightly, but he couldn't quite hide the

5

bitterness behind his words.

"I'm sorry." To me *Exodus* was just a story of something that happened years ago. To him it was obviously a lot more.

* * *

"Phone call for Dixie." The shouted words overpowered what passed for quiet hours in the second-floor hallway of the woman's dorm. The girl on phone duty was supposed to knock on the door of the girl getting a call, but trotting up and down the hallway for the daily two-hour study time was more than anyone could take.

I raced toward the telephone and stopped to take a calming deep breath before speaking. "Hello?" Happily, my voice did not come out a surprised squeak, and it pleased me not to hear the nervous waver I heard whenever I had to make a presentation in class.

"Hi, Dixie, this is Muhammad. I don't know if you remember…"

Remember? How could I forget? "I remember."

That call changed my life forever. Muhammad with the amazing brown eyes asked me on a date. A date! With those eyes! And what a date it was.

The preparations started early on the appointed day as I wrestled my stick-straight hair onto rollers. I turned my attention to advanced calculus homework while my hair dried. Later, I ironed out any closet wrinkles from my emerald green dress. The full skirt and the waist-length form-fitted jacket with the huge boat-neck collar were all designed to accentuate my tiny waist.

"We're going to a German Club dinner?" I asked as we walked across campus. "Will people be speaking German?"

"Some of them might."

"Do you speak German?" His easy laugh told me he didn't.

"I barely passed my foreign language requirement in German, even with a dictionary."

I had trouble keeping all my questions from popping out. Why were we going to a German dinner if we didn't speak German? Why was he required to take German for a degree in political science? Why did he ask me instead of some glamorous German girl? Somehow, I managed not to ask any of them. I had the feeling I was playing out of my league, and I was happy to let Muhammad fill the gap.

"As the president of the Foreign Student Organization, I go to as many of the foreign students' functions as I can. Theoretically, all foreign students belong to the F.S.O., but in reality, it acts as the umbrella organization of all the other clubs like the Latin Club, the French Club, Indian Student Organization, and so on. Believe me, the University of Florida has a lot of foreign students from a lot of different places. The clubs keep them feeling connected to home. The F.S.O. doesn't do much on its own. We mainly try to help with common problems and work with the Foreign Student Advisor."

As we entered the room, several people called to Muhammad, inviting us to sit with them. He steered me to a table and introduced the two men already sitting there to me. "This is Adnan Aswad from Syria." My hand was almost lost in the large, but thankfully gentle handshake. "And this is his brother, Herr Schwartz from Germany." Bewildered, I shook the other hand and settled into the chair Muhammad was holding for me.

"You're brothers?" Nods and grins from the men. "From two different continents?" They didn't look much like brothers. All three men laughed as though I had told a good joke.

"Our last names are the same, so we must be brothers." Adnan was laughing so hard he could hardly talk.

"Schwartz means black in German, and Aswad means black in Arabic," explained Muhammad. And thus I plunged headlong into the world of foreign students—almost all of whom were men working on doctorates. As a

7

lowly undergraduate, I was awed by their understanding of the world, and it was a big wide world, very unlike the one I knew.

Four months later Muhammad and I were married in a small civil ceremony in Grandmother Lola's living room.

* * *

I had considered myself reasonably sophisticated. My dad was military, and I'd lived up and down both coasts, and even spent freshman year of high school in Japan and a summer in Mexico. I soon realized I had been traveling inside a bubble of society that consisted of people very similar to myself. As a young girl of twenty, blinded by love and chock full of naïveté, I never considered the consequences of a cross-cultural marriage. Consequences that changed me in ways I could never have imagined.

The learning curve was steep, with plenty of slippery areas very early in the adventure. The marriage was not even a week old when I learned that food meant a lot more than a full stomach. More than just what you eat, food embodies attitudes, values, norms, and culture. It was a lesson that was not learned with one telling.

My first lesson in the cultural differences of food was the morning I "fixed breakfast" by setting out bowls, spoons, milk, and a choice of cereals. My thoughts of cereal were linked with memories of childhood when the sugary brands were rare treats, or bribes to eat fast and not miss the school bus.

"Do you want an egg?" asked Muhammad as he walked into the kitchen and pulled a frying pan out of the cupboard.

"I thought we'd have cereal for breakfast."

"Great. Cereal would be nice with an egg and toast."

"I was thinking we'd have cereal for breakfast today."

"You mean cereal instead of breakfast?"

"Cereal is breakfast."

"Really?" His muffled voice floated from the other side

of the refrigerator door. He emerged, triumphantly holding up the egg carton. "Haven't you ever heard that breakfast is the most important meal of the day?"

"Cereal isn't important enough?"

His quick laugh answered that question. "Breakfast should be something that opens the appetite. It should prepare you for the day in the best spirits." He placed the frying pan on the stove with a flourish and a wink. "You're going to love breakfast in Palestine."

I was happy to accept an appetite that could be opened like a window. Anything that made my non-morning husband wink that early in the morning was a miracle. Breakfast became a meal of choices and an ever-changing array of new favorites.

* * *

We were both full time students the first year of marriage, and we supplemented Muhammad's fellowship by driving a hundred-mile paper route through rural central Florida surrounding Gainesville. The paper was an evening paper during the week, but the Sunday edition was ready to be picked up in the early hours of the morning. More than once we went straight from a party to the newspaper office to pick up our papers. Then we'd go home and change our clothes for the long dark drive. I often packed peeled raw carrots. I worried that Muhammad might fall asleep on the drive home. When I felt my own head nod and my eyes close, I would bring out the carrots. It's not possible to fall asleep while eating raw carrots. They're just too noisy.

After we crunched through the carrots, I'd turn to Muhammad and ask him to tell me more about Palestine. His passion would get fired up and we'd have a lively ride home. Some weeks I'd ask about the history, always inseparable from politics. Other weeks I'd ask about his family. I'd known from the beginning of our relationship that his intention was to return home, and I wanted to be prepared.

I ran across a book in the library written by a woman telling what she went through when she moved "over there" with the husband she had met while he was studying in the U S. I couldn't believe my luck. I'd found a book that would tell me exactly what I needed to know.

Once I started reading, I couldn't put it down. I had it in my lap that afternoon as I rolled newspapers and snapped a rubber band around each one so Muhammad could toss them out of the car window onto the correct yard. After the papers were delivered, I continued to read on the drive home, mesmerized by the narrative. This sounded a lot more complicated than Muhammad made it seem. That night after kitchen chores and assignments for classes, we sat in bed reading as we often did.

"Muhammad, will I have my own dishes when we go to Palestine?"

"Of course you'll have your own dishes. Just like you have your own dishes here. Well, some of them weren't always yours, but they are now."

His little joke made me smile, in spite of my worry. He was referring to the dishes and tableware that a couple of dinner guests had brought with them from the university dining hall. When we moved into our apartment, we'd had only two of everything from Muhammad's bachelor days.

"That's not what I mean. The woman in this book had her own dishes in her in-laws' house. She didn't eat or drink out of anyone else's dishes because they would've had to break them and throw them away."

"What? Why?"

"Because she was a Christian. The dishes were apparently contaminated after she used them. It got too expensive to break everything she ate from, so they bought her dishes no one else used. Will your family break a glass if I drink out of it?"

"What are you reading?" He took the book out of my

10

hand. "This was published fifty years ago, and it must have happened fifty years before that in some backwater village somewhere. I never heard of such nonsense."

"But it's a Muslim country."

"Islam is a religion, not a guarantee against superstition or stupidity."

"But—"

"Aren't there people in this country who believe bad things come in threes? Or black cats are bad luck?" I nodded slowly, wondering if I'd said anything about things coming in threes. I didn't *really* believe it, but it was still comforting if three bad things had already happened. "Does that mean all Christians believe bad things happen in threes or black cats are bad luck?"

"No."

"Palestinians have no prejudice against Christians. After all, Palestine is the birthplace of Christianity. We aren't prejudiced against Jews, either, in spite of what you read in all the wrong places. We *are* prejudiced against people stealing our land." He made a disgusted snort. "Throw this book away."

"I can't. We'd have to pay for it, or I couldn't graduate."

He dropped the book on the floor. "We can't have that happen, can we?" He set his own book aside and turned off the light. "Don't believe that nonsense. My family's going to love you."

* * *

Sunday breakfast was late and leisurely. Sometimes we returned from our paper route before the sun rose and just fell into bed. One Sunday I got the bright idea of bypassing the usual bacon and eggs or pancakes for French toast.

Muhammad sat at the table and looked at his plate. "This is what we're having for breakfast? Bread?"

Still proud of my accomplishment, I explained, "It's French toast."

11

"It's bread with syrup."

"No, it's French toast. Try it." In my mind that was an explanation. Everybody knows what French toast is, right? It takes a long time to get used to examining anything that follows the words "everybody knows," to form a habit of questioning assumptions of common knowledge.

"Calling it French doesn't make it gourmet. It's still just toast."

Disappointed, resentful, and fighting tears, I responded, "You would have been happy with an egg and toast with jam, wouldn't you? It's the same thing with the egg inside the bread and syrup instead of jam."

"Why didn't you say so?"

French toast became a favorite.

As we took those first steps together, we made many compromises, but breakfast always remained an important meal—one that we shared with family whenever possible, and often with friends.

* * *

Two years later, in October 1964, our son Ibrahim was born, and we became a family of three. Shortly thereafter, Muhammad learned that his advisor was leaving the University of Florida at the end of the school year. Under the dual pressures of fatherhood and the need to finish his dissertation, Muhammad reached out to his academic contacts. He was offered a temporary teaching position at the brand-new Florida Atlantic University. It was perfect.

For the past two years, we had spent many evenings in the public library recording United Nations voting data on paper "scorecards" as the raw data for Muhammad's dissertation. Part of the agreement with FAU was that computer-science students would code the information, transfer it to punch cards (yes, nothing but the latest technology), and tabulate the results.

Muhammad worked feverishly to meet his deadline.

12

Once the tome was written, we rented an IBM Selectric typewriter, bought boxes of paper and carbon paper, and began typing. Five copies with no mistakes. Using a fresh sheet of carbon paper on the last copy and moving the others forward kept the print even. We typed in turns. One typed and one slept with an occasional break for food. We made the deadline and Muhammad completed his doctorate.

After the ordeal of the dissertation, Muhammad got a "real" job teaching political science at Jacksonville University. Joan Carver, the same friend who suggested Muhammad apply for the position at the university, also recommended me to the headmistress of a private girls' school. Since my degree was in mathematics, not education, I needed to take education classes to maintain my temporary accreditation.

I took advantage of being a faculty wife, a title that made me feel like I was playing dress-up, and I registered for a course in child psychology and one in teaching reading. Both were classes that I thought might make me a better mother. The reading professor told us that we must emphasize the left to right direction in everything we did. Even toddlers would benefit from the pre-reading training. What would happen to my children when we moved to a country where reading was right to left?

I worried, but Muhammad told me children did that all the time. In Jordan, public schools teach English beginning in the fifth grade, and private schools often start much younger. No one has trouble writing in different directions. I had to admit that Muhammad's English was superb—both spoken and written. Our children would grow up in a blended household speaking two languages and writing in whichever direction they chose. I liked that idea.

I continued my struggle to understand the culture which produced my new husband as well as his view of my culture, and along the way I discovered that culture is inextricably bound not only to language but also to food.

13

Food is precious. Not mere fuel for the body, it is a major pillar of the social ritual.

FRENCH TOAST

It's not surprising that French toast is no more French than French fries. In fact, it's been around a lot longer than the country. Bread soaked in a mixture of milk and eggs, then fried was enjoyed in the Roman Empire as early as the 5th century AD and called *pan dolcis*.[1]

The French eat a similar dish and call it *pain perdu* or lost bread because it is a good way of using stale bread. One story about the name is that an innkeeper named Joseph French put his version of the dish on his menu in 1724 and called it French Toast, not being well acquainted with the use of the apostrophe.[2]

When I make French toast, I use either French or Italian bread cut thicker than ordinary sliced bread. If I am using baguette, I cut it on an angle for a more attractive slice. Over the years I have tweaked my own method of making French toast with the addition of turmeric and cinnamon to the egg mixture and put even more cinnamon on top with a sprinkling of powdered sugar.

Both cinnamon and turmeric are powerful antioxidants, and they both have anti-inflammatory properties.[3] Cinnamon is a spice that I use generously in both sweet and savory dishes. The smell and taste enhance the flavors of meat and egg dishes, and it never seems out of place.

Turmeric has similar properties to cinnamon and has been the subject of considerable serious research. The active ingredient in turmeric is curcumin, which research has shown may be useful for wound healing and pain reduction.

Studies have shown that it may be effective in treating and preventing chronic diseases such as cancer, heart disease, and diabetes.[4]

However, turmeric is not easily absorbed by the body. Combining turmeric with fat helps the body absorb it, so its addition to fried food such as French toast is especially helpful.

Today many people worry about the calories in French toast and the cholesterol in the egg. Try using egg white instead of whole egg and substituting almond milk for regular milk.

Photo by Gail from flicker via Wylio.com

[1] https://thebreakfastshoppe.com/history-french-toast/
[2] https://www.neatorama.com/neatolicious/2013/10/17/French-Toast-Isnt-French-Heres-How-It-Got-Its-Name/
[3] https://cleanplates.com/know/nutrition/why-you-should-add-cinnamon-to-everything-you-eat/
[4] https://pubmed.ncbi.nlm.nih.gov/19233493/

Tea or Coffee?

Muhammad followed the rising tensions between Israel and the neighboring Arab countries. The Middle East began appearing in the news regularly as the situation grew more heated, and Muhammad gained a modest reputation as a speaker on the origins and ongoing progress of the conflict. The local Ramallah Club, whose members were all from the Palestinian city of Ramallah or descendants of immigrants from Ramallah, respected Muhammad's expertise and invited him to join—an unprecedented honor since he was from another region of the country.

It astounded me when we received several anonymous hate-filled telephone calls after he appeared on a local television program. While neither of us felt threatened, Muhammad was restless and feeling increasingly alienated. It was time to go home.

We began planning. I wanted to bring everything with me. Muhammad convinced me that furniture and appliances were best replaced, but I had to bring my bone china, didn't I? And the books. Both Muhammad and I had been collecting books for years. There was no way to take them on an airplane. A travel agent found a ship that would take us to Aqaba and the allowance for personal luggage was generous. I applied for a passport that included Ibrahim. We were scheduled to leave at the end of the school year.

However, the fates had other plans for us.

* * *

Gamal Abdel Nasser, the very popular President of Egypt, had been calling for Arab unity since his election in 1956. The

16

main rallying point was the defense of Palestine. In 1964 the League of Arab States voted unanimously to establish the United Arab Command, which raised tensions another notch. As time passed, Nasser came under increasing pressure to confront Israel. By 1967, he was speaking openly of attacking Israel, counting on the support of the other Arab nations.

June 5, 1967, in a pre-emptive strike, Israel destroyed most of Egypt's air force on the ground. The following day, Jordan invited Iraqi troops and armored units into Jordan.

Muhammad spent hours glued to the short-wave radio, listening to newscasts from all over the world, trying to separate fact from fiction, reporting from rumor. The news was not good. According to all reports, the Jordanian army was taking heavy casualties. Muhammad's only brother was an officer in the Arab Legion, the army of Jordan. Rumors spread and grew in the telling. We sent telegraphs with pre-paid replies asking for news of the family. Nothing. The more we heard, the more we worried. If the reports were true, entire units were being annihilated—especially ground troops. Muhammad reached out to our friends from Ramallah. "They know people. They have contacts."

Two days later, I came back into the living room after putting Ibrahim to bed. Muhammad was sitting with silent tears running down his cheeks. I ached with his pain. I sat and put my arms around him. There were no words. He was mourning. We sat with our arms around each other for a long time before he broke the silence.

"Everyone believes my brother's unit is gone." I tightened my hold on him. After another lengthy pause he continued, sentences separated by sad silences. I realized he was reorganizing his thoughts and planning as he spoke. "They took my hometown, Qalqiliya. No one knows what's happening there. My father may be there, stuck on the wrong side of the new border." Questions bubbled up in my head, but I left them unsaid. "My brother's family has no

17

one. A wife and ten children with no one to take care of them. And Yousef, his oldest son, is studying in Yugoslavia." He kissed the top of my head. "Moving overseas with no jobs is no longer an option. We have to cancel our plans or at least delay them indefinitely."

"Yes," I whispered, hoping he could feel my nod against his chest. I didn't want to interrupt the thoughts or intrude on his mourning of his brother.

"We need to make sure we have enough income to help. I don't know if Jordan makes any provisions for the families of soldiers." He took his arm off my shoulders and sat up straight. "Can you bring the checkbook?"

Stunned by the thought of supporting so many people, I brought the checkbook. "If they didn't get telegrams, how will they get checks?"

"This isn't for Jordan. I'll mail a check to Yusef tomorrow morning. He'll be stranded without money from home."

"Right." I was embarrassed that I hadn't even thought about Yusef.

"Can you talk to the headmistress tomorrow and see if she's filled your position for next year or if you can renew? I'll cancel our reservations and renew my own contract. The semester will be over in another week, and I've already bowed out of summer school. I'll leave as soon as I turn in my grades. You follow when you get your passport."

"Yes." Alone? Without him? I've never gone anywhere alone. My misgivings were masked by a nod.

"We'll never find out what they need from here."

Luckily, we were both able to renew our teaching contracts for the following school year.

True to his word, as soon as Muhammad's teaching duties were over, he tried to get a plane ticket home. No planes were flying into the area. The closest he could get was Greece.

"All right. Give me a ticket to Athens. I'll get a bus from

18

there. I'll buy a bicycle if I have to, but I have to take care of my family." Luckily, by the time he landed in Athens, the first planes were taking off for Lebanon. It was only a Six Day War, but in those six days Israel tripled its territory.

Only a Six Day War, but the consequences for Palestine were far reaching. Only a six day war, but Israel now held the entirety of Palestinian land, albeit much of it under military occupation. Only a six day war, but it created a second refugee population of over 300,000 people, many of whom were fleeing for a second time. Only a six day war, but Muhammad had forever lost his right to live in his ancestral home or eat the fruit grown in his grandmother's garden.

* * *

I followed as soon as I received my passport. I took my small son on the first flight I could find, carrying a passport with a large purple stamp on the first page that said it was not valid for travel to any of the countries in or near my destination. When it first arrived, I was shocked.

Luckily, before my shock turned into panic, I turned the page and found another stamp saying I could go. I was allowed one round trip to Jordan. That was it. Why was the stamp dated mid-May and we were now in mid-June? I was so grateful to be on my way that I didn't dwell on the question. I just started packing.

It was the first time I had even been in a plane without my parents—and I was flying right into a war zone.

We landed in Beirut, and the plane taxied down a runway lined with soldiers, a stark reminder that the airport had only reopened a few days ago. After deplaning, I scanned the crowd of people greeting the plane for a familiar face. Blissfully ignorant of the hassle involved in most border crossings, I had hoped Muhammad would take the nearly five-hour drive to meet us in Beirut. Disappointed, I bought tickets on the connecting flight to Amman.

My previous experience with borders had been limited to the Canada-US border, the Mexico-US border, or traveling using military transportation. I had a lot to learn.

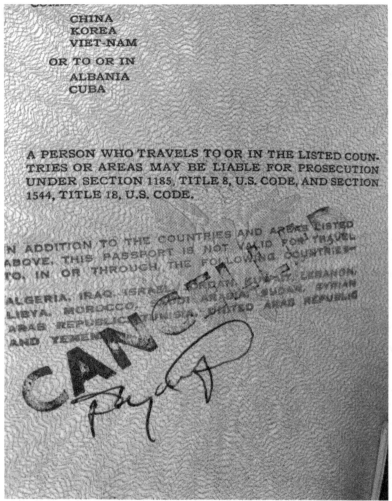

CHINA
KOREA
VIET-NAM

OR TO OR IN

ALBANIA
CUBA

A PERSON WHO TRAVELS TO OR IN THE LISTED COUNTRIES OR AREAS MAY BE LIABLE FOR PROSECUTION UNDER SECTION 1185, TITLE 8, U.S. CODE, AND SECTION 1544, TITLE 18, U.S. CODE.

IN ADDITION TO THE COUNTRIES AND AREAS LISTED ABOVE, THIS PASSPORT IS NOT VALID FOR TRAVEL TO, IN OR THROUGH THE FOLLOWING COUNTRIES:

ALGERIA, IRAQ, ISRAEL, JORDAN, KUWAIT, LEBANON, LIBYA, MOROCCO, SAUDI ARABIA, SUDAN, SYRIAN ARAB REPUBLIC, TUNISIA, UNITED ARAB REPUBLIC AND YEMEN.

The first list and paragraph quoting sections of legal code were printed on the original blank passport, the purple was a rubber stamp used on my passport. The large CANCELLED was added when the passport expired and was replaced.

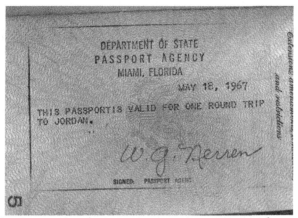

The date on the photo suggests pre-knowledge of the war that had not yet begun. Apparently, our State Department was not as surprised as the Egyptian Air Force.

Our plane to Amman was five hours late arriving from Paris, and we, along with the other six or seven people headed for Jordan, were escorted to a lounge with a bar.

Every doorway in the airport, exterior or interior, was guarded by at least two fully armed Lebanese soldiers. Each time we went through a doorway, our escort explained to soldiers at the door who we were and where we were going before we were allowed to pass.

As we were being herded through the nearly empty airport, we passed a window and I saw a group of olive-green tents with the familiar Palestinian flag flying in the center. I asked our escort who said it was a hospital for wounded fighters. Days later Muhammad explained that Lebanon was not actively engaged in the war, but as part of the United Arab Command they were technically at war with Israel.

After a couple of hours in the bar, we were escorted to an airport restaurant overlooking the runways and served dinner. The meal was strangely silent.

During the meal we lost electricity several times for short periods and sat in total darkness. Even the runway lights went dark until the electricity came back on. Were they blacking out the airport because war planes were still flying overhead? Or was their electricity that unreliable? Either way, it did not build confidence.

The five-hour wait stretched into an eternity of wondering if my husband received my telegram. What would I do if he didn't get it? I couldn't even get a cab from the airport because I didn't have a proper address.

At last the plane was ready to board. It was almost midnight. I had been traveling for twenty-three hours and I wasn't thinking straight. I sat down in my assigned seat, and it was wet. Maybe the plane leaked. How bad would that be if we went up and didn't have enough air pressure? The plane was nearly empty. I could have changed seats, but that didn't enter my befuddled, sleep-deprived mind. Luckily, I had little more than an hour to worry.

* * *

"We found him! We found our daddy!" Ibrahim yanked his hand out of mine and went running. Sure enough, we had found him. Muhammad scooped his son up in his arms and rushed toward me. It looked to me as though all the people waiting for the plane surged toward me from behind him. A handsome man in uniform stood beside him with a huge grin on his face. No one could mistake the resemblance. My eyes stung with tears. Muhammad's brother was alive!

"This is Abu Yusef, my brother. Give him your passport and baggage claim checks." Confused, I handed over the documents as requested.

"You have two brothers in the army?" I whispered to Muhammad after Abu Yusef disappeared.

"I only have one brother."

"Isn't his name Saleh?"

"Yes, but…" At this point the other people had crowded around us so tightly I was feeling claustrophobic. "I'll explain later." He turned to a man next to him who was

22

wearing traditional clothes. "This is my father."

I wasn't sure what to do. I couldn't hug such a dignified and imposing man. I extended my hand, and we exchanged a hearty handshake that nearly crushed a couple of my fingers. He said something and put his free hand over his heart. I decided my smile had to make up for my lack of words.

From there, the introductions continued. "Are all of these people family?" I managed to ask between cousins. "I'll never remember them all."

"It's all right."

Before we reached the end of cousins, uncles, nieces, nephews, and who knows what else, Abu Yusef came back with my suitcase and all the appropriate stamps on my passport.

"I didn't go through customs." I had seen the sign, and all the other passengers had disappeared.

"It's all about who you know," said Muhammad as we moved toward the exit.

"Do you know where the ladies room is?"

"Wait until we get to my sister's house."

"I've been waiting since Beirut. Ibrahim was tired and clingy."

"Wait. You don't want to use the bathroom here." He took my elbow and the entire crowd walked out of the terminal and filled most of the cars in the parking lot.

"Why did they all come to the airport?"

"To greet you. This is the first time you're visiting us."

"They came to stare at the blue-eyed wife?"

"No." He sounded offended. "They came to welcome you into the family. They consider you worth coming out in the wee hours of the morning. It's a sign of respect and caring."

"I'm truly honored, but they will think a lot less of me if I don't get to a bathroom soon."

"Wait. It won't be much longer."

23

I waited, but by the time we reached his sister's house (more cousins, more introductions), I was desperate. He got some tissues out of a box on a table and shoved them at me.

"I don't have to blow my nose. I have to pee."

"Take the tissues." It was a command. I took the tissues. He pointed down a hallway. Following the pointed finger, I found a bathroom, but there was no toilet—only what looked a little like a toilet bowl set into the floor. I was in far too much of a hurry to go ask for instructions. By the time I realized I was at the wrong angle, it was too late to correct my stance. I rejoined the family, feeling greatly relieved and praying I didn't smell like splashed pee.

We sat around the living room in chairs lined up along the walls to accommodate as many people as possible, and all the chairs were taken. We were served sweet tea out of little glasses.

"Um Abdullah," Muhammad said, "My wife drinks her tea without sugar."

"No sugar?" his sister echoed his words. "Not even just a little bit?" She sent her daughter to the kitchen to make my tea. "Does she use saccharine? Does she have diabetes?"

"No. She just likes it without sugar." They had never met anyone who drank tea without sugar. How was I ever going to fit into this family? I'd only been here for minutes and I was making trouble and sticking out like a sore thumb.

I drank my tea as conversation swirled around me. It was impossible to be attentive when I knew only a dozen words of Arabic. They had nearly exhausted my vocabulary in the first five minutes: welcome, tea or coffee, and sugar. Oh, yes, and his sister had called me Sweetheart. I was waiting to hear someone round out the set with Good Night. Why weren't we in bed yet?

An hour later, we piled back in a car for the half-hour ride to his brother's house where we would be staying. During the car ride, he explained the puzzle of the names.

"It's a sign of respect to address adults as Abu, father, or

24

Um, mother, followed by the name of their eldest son. It is an acknowledgement of their status as adults and contributing members of society. Using a person's given name is a familiar form and seldom used outside the family."

"So, you called your sister Um Abdullah even though her name is Zahara." I was hoping I had it right. My brain was beyond befuddled at this point.

He nodded. "That's right."

"So everybody has a given name and a 'parent of' name?"

"Not everyone uses what you call the 'parent of' name. Some people have dropped the custom and probably consider it old-fashioned or a peasant custom. Our family pretty much adheres to the practice."

"So that makes me…"

"Um Ibrahim."

"I don't think I like being called by my son's name. It's as though I'm nothing but a son maker, and my only reason for existence is to make you a son."

"That's not true. You don't want every Tom, Dick, or Ahmed calling you Dixie. It wouldn't be respectful."

"What's wrong with Mrs. Hallaj, or whatever the Arabic equivalent is?"

"Nothing's wrong with it, but it would make people feel like servants if they called you that. It's too formal for everyday use. Um Ibrahim is an intermediate between 'Hey, you' and 'Your majesty.'"

I was too tired to argue.

It had been well past midnight when our plane landed, and now I was dizzy with lack of sleep. Just when I thought I might close my eyes for the rest of the trip, the car stopped. We had arrived at Abu Yusef's house.

Um Yusef greeted me with a bear hug and a shower of kisses on both cheeks. She was wearing a very modest long-sleeved, floor-length nightgown—fire engine red! I loved

25

her instantly. She'd already accepted me as family, or she would have been dressed. That red nightgown set the beginning of a close and wonderful relationship.

* * *

Our summer visit ended all too soon, and we returned to our teaching jobs in the U S. I don't know if Muhammad ever told his brother that we had renewed our contracts in order to support his family if the need arose. I was never told any details about Abu Yusef's experience during the Six Day War, but I did learn that their father and his wife had walked for days from their home in Qalqilya to Amman with exactly the same thought: Abu Yusef's fate was unknown, and the family needed support.

The following summer Muhammad returned to visit his brother, but I was expecting our second child and did not accompany him.

It was to be three years before we moved to Jordan—just in time for a civil war called Black September.

If you want to learn more about Black September, try these YouTube videos:
(1) http://bit.ly/PalBegin1
(2) http://bit.ly/PalBegin2

TEA AND COFFEE

The idea that the world can be divided between tea drinkers and coffee drinkers is surprisingly common. My admittedly limited experience indicates that most people who enjoy one will also enjoy the other, assuming both are available.

In our house, it depended on the circumstances. Some meals seem to go better with one over the other. Choosing coffee or tea is far easier than pairing wine with cheese, especially for breakfast. For example, coffee seems perfect for a breakfast of pancakes, while tea works well with hummus.

The choice of beverage I offered my guests depended on the guest, the type of visit, the accompanying food, if any. I always had tea, coffee, and *qahweh*. The tea was served in small, clear glasses; the coffee was served as I would serve it in the States, in either a cup and saucer or a mug. Adding the word *qahweh*, implied that the coffee was American style. *Qahweh* was sweet and strong, made with coffee ground very fine, and served in small demitasse cups.

In my house, everyone added their own sugar to the tea, but most often the tea was sweetened in the pot. Sometimes mint or sage or chamomile was added to the teapot as well, but if guests were present, one always asked the guests' preferences first.

Tea and coffee both came to the Arab world long before they were known in Europe, although tea is many centuries older than coffee.

Tea was known in China as early as the tenth century BC. It began as a medicinal drink, but its use as a popular beverage was documented by the second century BC. By the third century AD it had become China's number one beverage.[1]

By the eighth century, China was trading tea to, among others, the Arabs. Tea was a commonly traded item along the silk road. It was not until the 16th century that it reached Europe, and another century before the British were introduced to tea.[2]

Historical records show the presence of tea drinking in India since 750 BC. Indians have their own origin story that Bodhidharma, the founder of Zen Buddhism, took the leaves to China in the 6th century BC. However, it was the British

27

who rediscovered and commercialized it.[5] The British also introduced the habit of drinking endless cups of tea.[6] India was the leading producer of tea for over a century until China passed it.[5]

Coffee, on the other hand, was not discovered until 1400 when, according to legend, an Ethiopian shepherd noticed his goats cavorting and full of energy after eating the red berries. The goats also did not sleep that night. The shepherd tried the beans with similar effect.[3,4]

The first reports of coffee used as a beverage is in the Sufi monasteries of Yemen, where it soon spread to the Mecca and Medina, and hence to the rest of the Middle East.[4]

The modern practice of roasting the beans originated in Arabia. Roasting or boiling then parching the beans, made them infertile, allowing the Arabs to keep a monopoly on the coffee crops until the 1600s.[3] The word "coffee" was derived from the Arabic qahweh, although it had to pass through the Turkish variation, kahveh, and the Dutch version, koffie before coming to rest as coffee.[3, 4]

Tea claims the top spot for most consumed beverage worldwide, but coffee holds second place as the most valuable legally traded commodity in the world. Oil is in first place.[3]

(1) https://tea101.teabox.com/history-of-tea/

(2) https://en.wikipedia.org/wiki/History_of_tea

(3) https://www.pbs.org/food/the-history-kitchen/history-coffee/

(4) https://en.wikipedia.org/wiki/History_of_coffee

(5) https://teacoffeespiceofindia.com/tea/tea-origin/

(6) https://www.financialexpress.com/lifestyle/tracing-the-history-of-chai-and-indian-and-chinese-claims-on-the-culture-of-drinking-tea/1753034/

HEALTH BENEFITS

Both tea and coffee boast of the many health benefits that accrue from their consumption. Many of the benefits, such as enhanced alertness, improved athletic performance, elevated mood, and increased metabolism, emanate from the caffeine that gives both drinks their invigorating qualities.[1]

The same caffeine that gives so many health benefits also causes health warnings. Taken in excess (over 400 milligrams) caffeine can cause insomnia and restlessness and, in extreme circumstances, can cause death.[2]

Generally, one cup of coffee has about 100 milligrams of caffeine, while one cup of black long-brewed tea has about 60. Green tea has roughly half the caffeine of black, and many herbal teas have little to no caffeine. All of these figures are approximations since variation in amount of tea or coffee used in brewing, water temperature, time brewing, method of preparation, all yield different results.[1]

The claims of health benefits for tea, while overlapping those of coffee, are far more extensive. The Tea Association of the U.S.A. presents a well-documented fact sheet that includes studies showing benefits in reducing the risk of heart attack, stroke, certain cancers, and neurological decline.[3] I found the studies showing links between tea drinking and reduced risk of dementia, Alzheimer's, and Parkinson's disease particularly surprising.

---

[1] healthline.com/nutrition/caffeine-in-tea-vs-coffee

[2] https://blog.warriorcoffee.com/blog/12-health-benefits-and-6-disadvantages-of-coffee-smashing-it

[3] www.teausa.com/teausa/images/Tea_Fact_Sheet_2019_-_2020._PCI_update_3.12.2020.pdf

[4] http://www.teausa.com/teausa/images/Tea_Fact_Sheet_2019_-_2020._PCI_update_3.12.2020.pdf

TEA TRADITIONS

In many countries, tea is more than just a beverage. It is often deeply connected with the culture and the people. Since tea originated in China as a medicinal herb, it is no surprise that Chinese tea ceremonies are a blend of philosophies: Confucianism, Taoism, and Buddhism reflecting respect of nature and search for peace.[1]

From China, tea drinking spread to Japan and Korea, both of which developed highly spiritual ceremonies of their own. The Japanese use powdered macha tea, a highly caffeinated green tea, in their ceremonies.[2]

Afternoon tea is now considered one of Great Britain's quintessential customs, initially practiced only by the upper classes. "Anna, Duchess of Bedford, is credited with creating *Afternoon Tea* in 1840, when she began taking tea with a light snack around 4:00 p.m. to ward off 'that sinking feeling.'"[3]

Tea was popularized and promoted by the temperance movement. High tea, although it sounds aristocratic, was initially served around six by the laborers and miners when they came home from work along with a more substantial meal than afternoon tea.[4]

India favors chai, a mixture of spices steeped into black tea and then brewed again with milk and sugar. The spices include cinnamon, cardamom, ginger, cloves, and black pepper. Chai has become the national drink in India. Even though India is a major producer of tea, almost 70% of the production is consumed domestically.[1]

Russia, too, has a tea culture. Tea was brought to Russia by the Mongols in the 17th century. Russian Caravan tea, the most commonly used, has a smoky flavor which originally developed during the eighteen-month caravan journey from China, but today fermentation gives it the flavor.[1]

The brewing is done with a quantity of tea in a small

ceramic pot. Each person pours a small amount of the tea concentrate into their cup and adds hot water from a tap on the *samovar*.[1] Traditionally, the samovar had a pipe-like chimney running through it providing a hot surface for the surrounding water. The chimney was heated by fire either within the pot or directly beneath it.[5]

The Arab World has its tea traditions as well, many as old as the drink itself. Not surprising in a region encompassing twenty-two countries and at least 425 billion people, the tea traditions do not extend to all communities equally. Only one aspect of tea drinking is common throughout the Arab world, and that is the concept of hospitality.

Arabs take hospitality very seriously. According to tradition, a guest is treated with honor, dignity, and respect. Guests are given the best cut of meat, are served first, given the best of everything the host can offer.

The importance of hospitality probably became part of the culture among the desert nomadic tribes or Bedouins. The extreme conditions of the desert make the existence of a "peace pact" an essential survival aspect in cases of chance encounters. The following story is well known, and is one of the first things Muhammad told me when explaining the customs and guiding me toward the proper responses:

> In the desert, hospitality has been commonly understood to extend for three full days. Being under a man's roof also means, to the Badu (Bedouins), being in their protection. Among the famous incidents in Arab folklore is that of a man who took refuge, unwittingly, in the tent of a shaikh whose son he had just killed. Even under these circumstances the sacred law of protection was observed. Not until three days had passed, at which time the guest was obliged by custom to depart, was the tribe free to go in pursuit and avenge the shaikh's dead son.[6]

"Do not admire anything in the house like a vase or tray or picture. If you admire it, they will have to give it to you." I learned that hospitality has both rights and responsibilities. The guest, in turn is obliged to spare his host inconvenience whenever possible.[6]

---

[1] https://www.internations.org/magazine/what-s-your-cup-of-tea-tea-cultures-around-the-world-19048

[2] healthline.com/nutrition/caffeine-in-tea-vs-coffee

[3] www.teausa.com/teausa/images/Tea_Fact_Sheet_2019_-_2020._PCI_update_3.12.2020.pdf

[4] https://www.afternoontoremember.com/learn/etiquette

[5] https://en.wikipedia.org/wiki/Samovar

[6]https://archive.aramcoworld.com/issue/196502/manners.in.the.middle.east.htm

Photo by Ali Sarvari via Unsplash   Photo by Emre Gencer via Unsplash

Tea leaves in Taiwan—Photo by tsaiga via unsplash

Photo by McKay Savage via flickr Arabica beans taken in Columbia

Coffee service for guests or family   Russian Samovar
Photo: Marie-Louise Karlsson-flickr   Photo: Benito Bonito via Wikipedia

Bread

There's nothing like the smell of fresh-baked bread. Even heavily laced with wood smoke, the smell made my mouth water. My sister-in-law crouched in the narrow space between the house and the wall separating their property from the neighbors. At one end of the space, pigeons hid in their tiny nesting boxes that reminded me of tenement houses. The other end held a jumble of things, probably years of "we'll fix that someday" things. She poked at a fire with a thick stick, inverted what looked like a wok over it, and slapped a round flat piece of dough on the hot iron. She reached behind her and pulled out a short three-legged stool. I thought she planned to sit on the stool, but when she beat on the stool with a small hatchet, I recognized the thick stick she used to poke the fire as the fourth leg of the stool. Sweat trickled down the side of her face as she fed the fire. I was in awe of her resourcefulness.

Couldn't she have made the bread on the stove in the kitchen? Oh, right, no one knows how long it will be before we can replenish the propane for the stove. Gas, like water and food, has to be conserved.

The wind shifted slightly, and wood smoke drifted into the house, making my eyes sting. I didn't understand her words, but her gestures commanded me to close the door. I did as I was told and leaned against the wall. The tears I fought to control were only partially caused by smoke.

Here I was, just two months in the country, and neither Muhammad nor I had found employment. To be fair, we wanted to find work, but job hunting was not possible.

35

Sporadic but unpredictable outbursts of gunfire had punctuated the previous two months, the sound of which would cause all public transportation to disappear immediately— worse than New York City in a snowstorm.

One of the consequences of the June War of 1967 was the addition of a well-armed and well-organized fighting force to the young Palestine Liberation Organization. The PLO conducted raids into Occupied Palestine, often from within Jordan. Under Israeli threats of retaliation and pressure from the United States, King Hussein demanded the withdrawal of the *fedayeen*, the PLO fighters, to areas well away from any population centers and a stop to the raids. The tension between the PLO and the government had been mounting steadily and clashes between them were increasing.

Was it only a week ago that I accompanied Feryal, a teenaged niece, to the market to buy vegetables? It seemed longer. I was enthralled with the sights and sounds—the smell of overripe fruit, the slippery feel of crushed vegetation under foot, the babble of voices as men and boys jostled hand carts between the stalls, delivering goods or offering their services to shoppers.

In the midst of shopping, we heard the now-familiar sound of automatic weapons. Feryal grabbed my hand and pulled me along, threading her way through the crowd and into a small alley. The market echoed with the rattle and bang of corrugated steel doors slamming over store fronts. In minutes the streets were empty. We moved quickly through narrow passageways, half running when we crossed wider streets, until we emerged, almost miraculously, across the street from our house.

A few days after the ill-fated shopping trip, just before dawn, Um Yusef, my sister-in-law came into our bedroom with tears running down her face. "Listen. It's started." I heard it. The machine gun bursts were almost continuous— some sounded far away, while others were alarmingly close. She pulled me to the window and pointed up. Streaks of yellow and orange crossed the black sky like stars falling up instead of down.

"Tracer bullets," explained my husband. "These are not hand weapons, but artillery fire."

"Why do they glow?"

"Every so many bullets there is one that flames. It helps them gauge the trajectory and fine-tune their aim." We watched in silence for several minutes. "It's official. The army is now involved." My heart leaped into my throat. His brother was an officer in the Jordanian army. No wonder Um Yusef was in tears. "I'm going to talk to Um Yusef. There's nothing you can do. Maybe you should go back to sleep."

I nodded, knowing I didn't have any words to comfort my sister-in-law—and it wasn't just my lack of Arabic vocabulary. Even though I wouldn't sleep, at least I wouldn't be in the way. As I turned toward the bed, I glanced at the mattress where the boys slept. There was one small lump under the cover. "Where's Ibrahim?" Before Muhammad could answer, we both heard the hinges screech on the heavy iron door that led outside. We almost collided in our mad rush out of the bedroom. Our five-year-old, Ibrahim, was halfway out the door in his bare feet and red-and-white-striped pajamas.

Muhammad scooped him up in one arm and slammed and locked the door with the other one. "Where do you think you're going?" His voice was low, trying not to wake anyone who might still be asleep, but worry and fear underlined each word with suppressed emotion.

"Outside to watch the fireworks. The window's too small, and I'm missing most of them."

Muhammad hugged him tighter. "It's still nighttime. Go back to bed with Mommy."

We made a quick detour to the bathroom, then I carried him back to the bedroom. I told him he could lie down in the big bed with me and face the window to watch for more fireworks. How do you explain a concept like civil war to a five-year-old? And there was no doubt about it, Jordan was now in the throes of a full-fledged civil war, soon to be dubbed Black September.

It didn't take long for the noise level outside our bedroom to indicate the family was up and starting the day. By the time I emerged, tanks were rumbling down the street in front of the house, and the gunfire was constant. Walking past the living room, I did a double take on seeing the room full of men I'd never seen before. It looked like a normal gathering of guests, but there was no conversation. A strange visit in the middle of a war. Muhammad caught sight of me and jumped up. He came out and steered me toward the kitchen.

"I wasn't going in."

"I just wanted to talk to you. Are you all right?"

"I'm fine."

"Are you sure you don't want me to send you back to your mother?" I rolled my eyes at him. Before we married, my mother had demanded he leave an open return ticket with her before taking me out of the country—just in case I needed to escape. It had become our little joke as we lightened stressful moments.

"We don't have a phone to call a cab for the airport." I gave him a playful poke. Moving closer to put my mouth near his ear, I asked, "Who are all those men? Why are they here...now?" I didn't want anyone to hear me being nosy, and the surrounding noise level was reaching tooth-rattling intensity. Besides, it was an excuse to be close.

"They're refugees from the neighboring buildings. We have the only one-story building around. People from the taller buildings think our house is safe because the other buildings protect it."

"How did they get here? There are tanks and people shooting out there."

"I think they climbed over the back wall and came through the side door."

"They're all men. Did they leave their wives at home? If the houses aren't safe, how could they leave their wives?"

"Maybe they sent their wives away before the fighting broke out. Maybe only the single men felt the need to leave the building. How do I know?"

None of that made sense to me, but I had other things on my mind.

There were no introductions, no generous hospitality— just a pitcher of drinking water and shelter from the chaos reigning outside in the streets. No one expected more. Neither electricity nor water were running. Like all houses in the area, we had a metal reservoir on the roof with water. If we were lucky, no bullets would pierce the sides. If we were lucky and careful, the family could manage for days, but I wasn't sure how much strain the additional men in the living room would put on the water supply.

After several hours, the fighting got close enough that we could distinguish the army weapons from those of the guerrilla fighters by sound alone. The house reverberated with heavy arms being fired far too close for comfort. Um Yousef announced that no one could go into the rooms that faced the street. She made Muhammad evacuate the living room and bring the men into the hall. With the bedroom our family was using, the entry way, and the living room declared off limits, I counted fifty people now crowded into the one remaining bedroom and the wide hallway that bisected the house. Most stared straight ahead, like passengers in a crowded elevator, trying to maintain the illusion of personal space.

Conversation was impossible. Even the children were subdued. Faisal, our two-year-old, had tired of running to the front door whenever a tank passed. "Bus! Bus!" He loved bus rides and couldn't understand why we were passing up so many opportunities. Ibrahim and his youngest cousin, only a few months apart in age, sat in a corner chattering together. We'd only been here a couple of months. How had

Ibrahim learned enough Arabic to chatter? Or was it some secret language that didn't need shared words to have meaning?

No one ever said it out loud, but we cycled through the kitchen in ones and twos around mealtime. It would have been the height of rudeness to serve a family meal in front of the neighbors, none of whom were friends, and many were not even nodding acquaintances. Who knew how long we would have to live on whatever supplies we had in the house?

Maybe I was in the kitchen grabbing a quick bite with the children because I didn't see the teacher and his family arrive. Um Yusef did not want them in the hall with all the men from the living room who were now sitting around on mats. She took the couple and their two children into the back bedroom with the family. The newcomers took over one of the single beds, crowding the many Hallajs into an even smaller space.

As a family, they were a disruptive influence. The teacher himself was a jellyfish, totally without backbone; his wife was a screamer, and his children (both preschool age) were constantly crying and trying to get under the bed. I didn't blame the kids. They watched their parents, and all they saw was fear and panic. Every time something exploded close enough for us to cringe from the volume of the blast or feel a vibration through the floor, the woman screamed out something. Her husband rocked and recited verses from the Koran, and the children cowered under the bed with cries and shrieks.

During one brief lull in the action, the teacher ventured to the front door and peeked out the small window. We all heard a loud explosion, and he came running back to the bedroom, his face white and his hands shaking. "There were snipers in the church bell tower. The army blew up the bell tower, and everyone was killed." His voice was shrill and unsteady.

About ten minutes later, Feryal came to us and whispered in her uncle's ear, "I just looked outside and the bell tower looks fine to me."

Muhammad got up and left the room. He was fighting to hide a smile when he sat down beside me again. "She's right. Can't even see a chip in the stone from this distance. There may have been snipers. It's a great location." He shrugged and gave me a grin. "Guess that's how stories of fire-breathing dragons and other monsters begin."

* * *

By the time we lit the kerosene lamps that night, I barely noticed the sounds of war all around us. It's strange how quickly people can get accustomed to difficult and abnormal circumstances. The teacher's kids came out from under the bed but were still clinging to their mother like limpets— whiney limpets. It wasn't hunger. Um Yusef had been slipping them sandwiches made with her homemade pita bread. We all ate sandwiches. They were just tired, frightened, and in a strange house surrounded by far too many people. I could relate.

The lone kerosene lamp threw crazy shadows on the walls every time someone moved. It gave me an idea. I asked for paper and scissors and cut out some crude figures and used the shadows to tell the "classic" story of the wicked landlord who threatened to throw the poor old lady into the street unless her beautiful daughter married him.

The little ones loved the shadows, and the voices I used for the characters. I think the older ones had more fun trying to follow the plot in spite of my clumsy attempts to tell the story in Arabic. My Arabic was still at the stage where I translated word for word from English—and I stopped the narrative every third word or so to get another word translated. At least the crazy foreign lady made everyone laugh for a few minutes, and the whiners drifted off to sleep.

41

* * *

That was two days ago. Today things had calmed down, and the neighborhood refugees had left the way they came. Now the bread was almost gone, and Um Yusef was crouched over a fire of broken furniture cooking one loaf of pita bread at a time, dark circles under her eyes from lack of sleep. I felt so guilty, so useless. Muhammad and I, along with our two boys made four more mouths for this wonderful woman to feed. Four more people taking valuable resources of food and water.

Water. I couldn't remember my last shower. Never mind. It was quiet today.

Maybe I'd get to sleep in the big bed tonight. I didn't want to spend another night in a single bed spooning with Ibrahim and searching for a place I could put my feet without kicking my husband or two-year-old son, sleeping with their heads at the other end of the bed. In truth, I had the better end of the deal. The two-year-old was a restless sleeper.

Comfortable beds and showers weren't the priority today. Bread was the priority. Last night Um Yusef had kneaded the dough and set it to rise. This morning, she rolled the dough and formed the loaves, which she set on wooden trays and covered with cloth to rise again. Normally one of the older girls took the tray to the local bakery and brought back fresh bread that filled the house with its aroma as it cooled. But today was anything but normal. The only people on the streets today were carrying guns. Um Yusef had found her own solution. Bread is a necessity. I'd found that out a few months into my marriage. The memory seemed like a story told by someone else. It came from a world of innocence and ignorance.

* * *

One night during our first month of marriage, I was particularly proud of the results of my daily struggle to put together a meal that tasted good and looked reasonably attractive. I called my husband to the table.

"Where's the bread?"

"We ate the last of it for lunch. I'll buy some tomorrow."

I sat speechless when he got up, grabbed the car keys, and drove off in search of bread. By the time he returned, the meal was cold, but I had dried my tears and learned a lesson about the importance of bread in my husband's mind. It is a lesson I have never forgotten.

Later that evening, he interrupted our study time with, "Did you know you can't get bread in Chinese restaurants?"

"I never thought about it one way or the other." And still not thinking about it, I thought as I tried to recapture the feel of the story I was reading. I had signed up for an elective in Children's Literature. My math major friends thought I was nuts, and the English majors taking the course agreed.

"When I first came to this country…"

"Yes?" I put my book down and smiled at him. I loved stories, and I'd already lost the thread of the one I was studying. Besides, the ones he told were different. His friends were different; his ideas were different; his way of talking was different. When he told stories, his voice had a cadence and a rhythm that entranced me. Not to mention that I still knew very little of his life before we met. Four months was precious little time to learn, but I had the rest of our lives to unwrap the mysteries.

"There were a handful of Arab students in my little junior college. All of us were recent arrivals—a little homesick and not very comfortable with English, so we stuck together outside of classes. Nothing was easy for us. The college was in a small town, and the people weren't used to hearing accents. I had to say everything two or three times before people understood what I wanted. Everything was foreign."

"No," I interrupted with a giggle. "Everything was normal. You were the ones that were foreign."

"Yeah, I guess, but we didn't see it that way."

"Uh-huh." If I hadn't already been in love with him, the grin he gave me then would have insured my fall.

"Anyway, we found this Chinese restaurant that had food we liked and could afford. We spent at least five minutes trying to order bread with our meal. At first, we thought it was our accents, because it often was. Then we understood. They just don't have bread in Chinese restaurants. After that we brought our own bread when we went there."

"You brought your own bread to a restaurant?" I was taken aback by the idea of bringing food to a restaurant. "And they were all right with that?"

"Not at first. Then we explained. 'Look. We're Arabs, and Arabs can't eat without bread. Either you let us bring our bread, or you sell us bread, or we go to another restaurant.' It was simple, really."

"So, they decided you could bring your own bread."

"The restaurant was never busy. People didn't go out to eat very often, and I guess small town America was pretty insular in their eating habits. After they got over the initial shock of a customer bringing food to a restaurant, they were all right with it. We came often and they welcomed the business." He paused, and I could see he was picturing the scene. "They started greeting us by asking if we remembered to bring our bread."

"I'm sorry you had to bring your own bread tonight."

"It's okay. You didn't know."

ABOUT BREAD

Today you will always find some store-bought pita and at

least one loaf of good Italian or French bread in my freezer.

It may be difficult for someone raised with today's supermarkets that carry food from around the globe, and with entire television stations devoted to food preparation, to understand how simple and even monotonous my American food was when I was growing up. I learned what little I knew about cooking while living in a family that ate a piece of meat (beef, pork, or chicken, and fish on Friday) accompanied by a serving of potatoes (boiled, mashed, or baked) along with a serving of vegetables from a can. Salad was rabbit food, and fresh fruit was expensive—hence rare. Bread was white and sliced. Although used mainly for sandwiches, it still had a place on the table. French bread was available but was not part of the daily fare.

I had never seen or heard of flat bread before I married a Palestinian—and, no, I wasn't living under a rock or in some isolated valley somewhere. I was part of mainstream America that based its idea of perfection on TV's Ozzie and Harriet Nelson.

Today pita bread can be found in all the major supermarket chains as well as in specialty shops. Fifty years ago, it was a delicacy found only in specialty stores, and we ate what we found on the shelves.

BREAD IN ARAB CULTURE

Bedouins refer to bread as *aish*, a word which also means life. For Arabs, bread is truly the staff of life. It is a staple for all Arabic meals, but breakfast in particular relies on bread. Without bread, there is no breakfast. Indeed, there is no meal, regardless of the time of day. It is no wonder that bread plays an important role in Arab culture. After all, wheat was first sown, tended, and reaped in the Middle East around 8,000 B.C.[1], and soon thereafter the Egyptians invented the first grinding stone.

45

The first bread was probably flat and unleavened, baked in underground ovens or on hot rocks. The principal attraction was the portability.[2] It is generally accepted that the warm climate of Egypt and the Egyptian skill in brewing beer led to the development of leavened flat bread, similar to today's Arabic breads around 3,000 B.C.[3] Is it any wonder that bread is a crucial part of Arab culture? It has been there from the beginning.

According to the Middle East Research and Information Project, it is estimated that the average person in Jordan consumes 198 pounds of bread per year.[4] Compare that with the 53 pounds that a report by Southern Utah University says the average American consumes. Arabs eat over three times the amount of bread eaten by Americans.[5]

The quantity of bread Arabs consume is only part of the answer to the importance of bread. Why is bread such a vital part of the diet? Perhaps because it was part of the culture centuries before Columbus sailed to the New World. In fact, bread was part of the culture long before Rome became the center of an empire.

Consider the lifestyle of the nomadic Bedouin. Bread is one of the most portable foods there is. What do we pack for picnics? What do we pack for lunch when we're off to work or school? Often, the answer is: sandwiches.

What makes sandwiches the perfect food on the go? Bread combines with other food is an easy-to-eat package that needs no tools or cutlery to eat. It would be a major pain to haul forks and spoons, bowls and dishes—not to mention the difficulty of using them on camel back or while trying to find shelter in a raging sandstorm.

Today the vast majority of Arabs live in regular houses with all the modern appliances we consider necessary, and some that are more compact and better engineered than the ones available here. They watch soap operas on television, put their children on school buses in the morning, go to work, shop in malls, attend movies, and so forth—yet the omnipresence of bread remains part of the culture itself.

Jordan started subsidizing bread in the sixties. They had bread riots in the seventies when they withdrew the subsidies. The subsidy was reinstated.[4] With the recent influx of refugees from Syria, the subsidy was endorsed by the World Bank as a measure crucial to the "uninterrupted provision of basic household commodities."[6]

An excellent article on Arabic bread, complete with recipes, explains that the soft and pliable qualities of the bread make it work. The bread can be dipped in liquid or semi-liquid foods; it is perfect to pick up chunks of meat, vegetables, finely chopped salads; it can be folded into a scoop to pick up anything in between.[7]

Bread can be the plate on which the meal is served. It can be the utensil with which the meal is eaten. It can also be the meal itself. Stale bread soaked in sweet tea has sustained many an Arab in difficult times.

Bread is life.

References for statistics and facts:
[1] bit.ly / PalBread1
[2] bit.ly / PalBread2
[3] bit.ly / PalBread3
[4] bit.ly / PalBread4
[5] bit.ly / PalBread5
[6] bit.ly / PalBread6
[7] bit.ly / PalBread7

* * *

Pita bread, also known as pocket bread, is the image that everyone thinks of when Arabic bread is mentioned. It is the most common type of bread in the Middle East, because it is the most versatile. Like all bread, it can be frozen for long periods and is still delicious when defrosted—and it stays fresh longer than thinner breads.

However, pita is not the only bread native to Palestine. Taboon (or tabun) bread is named after the domed stone ovens that villagers used to build. The ovens resemble stone igloos. On baking day, a fire is built inside the oven. As the fire subsides into embers, the village women slap the thin rounds of dough onto the oven walls. When the dough falls off the wall, the bread is baked. At least that is what I remember from a conversation with an elderly relative who lived in the tiny village of Burhaam.

Other sources refer to stones placed on the floor of the oven that give the bread its pebbly appearance. The DIY recipes depend on hot uneven baking surfaces.

The typical taboon loaf has a larger diameter than pita bread and does not have a pocket. Today there are other ways of getting results similar to taboon bread. In the story above, Um Yusef baked flat bread on an inverted wok over an open flame. Other methods use a baking sheet covered with pebbles or even glass beads to duplicate the texture of the original. Still another approach uses a large flat frying pan, flipping the dough when the bottom gets brownish dots.

Taboon bread is usually made with a combination of whole wheat and white flours, one part whole wheat to three or four white. Taboon bread has become more popular with the rising popularity of wraps, and something similar can often be purchased in specialty stores.

———————————

Instructions and recipes for homemade taboon bread:
[8] bit.ly / PalBread8
[9] bit.ly / PalBread9

MY EASY PATH TO HOMEMADE PITA

One of my daughters-in-law once telephoned me a few days before Thanksgiving. "I offered to cook Thanksgiving dinner for a few friends. It seemed like a good idea at the time, but now I'm looking at cookbooks and trying to make a list of ingredients. I haven't even started, and I'm overwhelmed. You've made Thanksgiving dinners for us for years and smiled through the whole ordeal. Any advice?"

I looked around the kitchen to make sure no one was listening, then I answered in my best conspiratorial voice. "I always buy a pre-stuffed Butterball turkey. It goes from freezer to oven. An hour before it's ready to come out, scrub some white and sweet potatoes, wrap them in foil, and pop them in the oven. Half an hour later, pop in the green bean casserole. Add rolls and cranberry sauce and you're done."

"Wow! I just knew if anyone had an easier way to do it, it would be my mother-in-law." I could hear the relief and laughter in her voice.

So, in an effort not to tarnish the reputation, I will tell you my secret path to pita. Bread dough is available in the freezer section of your local supermarket. One loaf of dough will make three to five small loaves of pita. Once the dough has thawed and doubled in size, divide into three to five equal parts. Form each part into a ball. Once all the balls are formed, coat the tops with a very thin layer of olive oil to keep them from sticking. Cover the batch with plastic and a clean cloth for about ten minutes. Flatten each ball and roll it out into disks. If you can get the disks about a quarter inch thick, that would be best. Sometimes I have trouble getting them that thin. Just make sure they're less than half an inch thick. Let the disks sit for another ten minutes.

From there you can use any of several methods to make the dough into bread. Some cooks prefer to cook them on top of the stove in a flat frying pan, others use a regular oven. I bake them for about 3 minutes in my Nuwave oven, flip and bake 2 or 3 more minutes on the other side. This is a longer bake time than many recipes, but my husband likes it to be brown and not doughy.

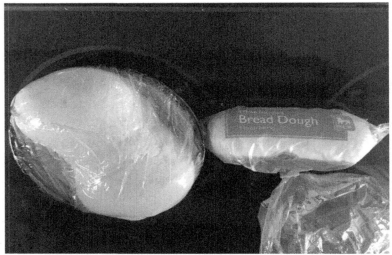

That's all there is to it!

The advantage to using a regular oven is that you can bake a small batch all at one time, but the oven must be very hot. I prefer to use the portable oven because I can see what is happening, and I have more control over the process. Yes, it takes longer. However, it doesn't require as high a heat and I don't get the blast of hot air in my face when I try to turn or look in on them.

Don't worry if you don't have a Nuwave oven, you can also use a regular oven, or even a flat frying pan. For examples, there are many excellent YouTube videos to guide you through it.

Try it yourself. The result is yummy, and it's fun to make.

Videos and recipes for homemade pita bread:
(10) bit.ly/PalBread10 uses a regular oven.

[11] bit.ly/PalBread11 a more complex recipe, using a non-stick frying pan.

[12] bit.ly/PalBread12 a recipe that includes some olive oil in the dough. He also grills the bread in a flat pan.

[13] bit.ly/PalBread13 uses an electric pot.

Labneh (Kefir Cheese)

The following day, Feryal surprised us all with a burst of laughter. She had the small radio pressed to her ear in order to hear over the sounds of guns and artillery, passing troop carriers and tanks.

"What's so funny?"

"The news just announced that law and order has been restored in Zarqa."

When the general laughter quieted, Muhammad translated the announcement for me.

"What's the point of that? Anyone who's conscious knows it's a lie."

"We know it's a lie because we live in Zarqa. The rest of the country will be inclined to believe it. Zarqa is an army town. If it's not quiet in Zarqa, then it's not quiet anywhere. The government is trying to break the morale of the PLO."

The noise level around our house gradually subsided over the next two days.

* * *

One rather quiet morning breakfast was served, as usual, on a collection of small plates. One plate grabbed my attention as a stray sunbeam turned the deep greenish-yellow extra virgin olive oil almost fluorescent and lit the brilliant white mounds that sat like islands in the shimmering sea. This was not the first morning we'd had labneh, but the beauty of the balls of yogurt based cheese swimming in the sunlit oil was breathtaking.

Like so many other things in this house, Um Yusef

53

made labneh from scratch. A gallon jar sat on her countertop, usually filled to the brim with white balls submerged in the local dark yellow virgin olive oil. Labneh balls keep indefinitely when surrounded by olive oil. The cheese was either served on a small plate with some olive oil and eaten much as hummus is, with bits of pita bread or spread on pita bread sandwich style.

Another small dish held a mound of jam. Homemade cucumber pickles were sliced and available on another. Not a big variety, but the bread made the meal. I was always aware of the effort Um Yusef made keeping us all in bread, and I worried about how long we would have to live off the stored supplies in the house. The huge sack of flour tucked away in the corner was visibly sagging. There must be a limit to the magic she could pull together in the kitchen. I kept my concerns to myself. Everyone knew, but no one said anything. I felt selfish worrying about my stomach while others worried about Abu Yusef. Would he survive this ordeal?

We settled into another day of sitting around, watching the children chatter in some undefined language that transcended the Arabic-English divide, and worrying. The fighting had moved on. The sounds of artillery and Kalashnikovs were distant enough that we no longer cowered in the back bedroom. Perhaps the fighters had left our section of the city. We went out into the enclosed courtyard and heard distant gunfire, which Muhammad said was coming from the vicinity of the refugee camp. Nothing had changed in the last few days. It seems strange to say, but I was bored.

Every time I tried to help in the kitchen, Um Yusef shooed me away, saying there were plenty of people in the small kitchen already. Um Yusef had eight daughters and two sons. The oldest, Yusef, the one we'd sent money to in 1967, was still studying in Yugoslavia. I wondered how he was managing now that neither his father nor his uncle sent money. I hoped he had made friends in the past few years who would see him through this crisis.

Muhammad's three oldest nieces had married in 1969, within four or five months of each other. Two were living in Amman in the same neighborhood as Muhammad's sister, each with a small infant. The third niece lived in Saudi Arabia where her husband, a Palestinian from Gaza, operated and half-owned a very successful car repair shop. The other half was owned by a Saudi businessman. Non-Saudis were forbidden to own their own businesses in the country.

Five girls and the younger boy, all still in school, lived in the two-bedroom house along with us in Zarqa. It was a remarkably harmonious household, considering how many people shared the space.

Looking around for something to pass the time, I followed my ears to find the source of a peculiar rattling sound. I found the older girls sitting in a circle on the bedroom floor, and the sound was coming from the center of the circle. They made room for me as I entered, and I sat in the circle. They were playing a variation of "Jacks." It amazed me that the game was nearly identical to the version played in my old schoolyard. The major difference was that they didn't spend money on store-bought games. The "jacks" were small stones, and they even tossed a stone up instead of a ball. It made the game much more difficult because, of course, the stone didn't bounce—leaving little time to pick up the needed number of stones. We all laughed at my attempts. Either my toss was wild, or I scattered the stones I tried to pick up while keeping my eye on the rapidly descending stone that I still thought of as a ball.

Muhammad poked his head into the room where I was struggling to control the small stones. It made a convenient excuse for me to get up without feeling like a quitter.

"What's up?"

"Follow me."

His terse reply reminded me of my mother's saying, "Little pitchers have big ears." Mystified, I followed him into the laundry/bathing room. The old wringer washing machine sat amidst various wash tubs and buckets on one side. The shower was on the other side, and a floor drain served them both. The toilet had its own little room and the washbasin was in an alcove off the common area.

I smelled smoke the minute I stepped into the room. Muhammad handed me a small towel. "Hold this over the window. I have to burn these papers, but I don't want smoke pouring out the window. A column of smoke coming out of a window will call the soldiers as clearly as an Indian smoke signal."

The single window in the room was set high above eye level. After all, it was a bathroom. I had to stretch my arms as high as I could reach to cover the window with the towel. "What are you burning?"

"Records. Names, identities." He fanned a small fire that was already smoldering in a bucket. I saw a stack of papers next to it on the floor.

"Where did they come from?"

"The neighbor lady brought them in a panic. The soldiers are searching house to house for contraband."

"Contraband?" The word made me think of smuggling. I knew people smuggled cigarettes from one country to another to avoid customs and taxes, but papers?

"Her son was in charge of the local youth group of Fatah."

"I see." Pieces fell into place. Fatah was the main branch of the Palestine Liberation Organization, or PLO. These were the freedom fighters that were being hunted down by the Jordanian Army. "And the papers?"

"The idiot kept a record of everyone. Pictures, names, addresses, everything."

"Where is he? Why isn't he doing this?" It was hot, and we were in a closed room with a fire. Sweat trickled from my armpits. I didn't try to hide the resentment. We hadn't had water for showers since the fighting started, and I was sweating like a pig, doing a job someone else should have done days ago.

"She hasn't seen him since the army got involved."

My resentment evaporated, unlike my sweat. "The poor woman. She doesn't know if he's out there fighting or..." My voice trailed off, unwilling to put my thoughts into words.

"He's probably holed up somewhere. I doubt if he's toting a Kalashnikov."

"Still, she must be worried sick."

"She's more worried about what will happen if the soldiers get their hands on these names and pictures. They won't only be looking for her son, they'll be looking for these kids—and their families."

"Why the families?"

"Families always get the blame for anything kids do. They'll assume the families have the same political opinions the kids have, and they'll probably be right. The fathers could go to jail or lose their jobs. Any number of things could go wrong." His voice caught and he coughed.

"Don't talk anymore." I felt the effects of the smoke in my own throat. I lifted the towel for a few seconds, watching to see how much smoke escaped and how visible it might be from another vantage point. We worked in silence for minutes. My stinging eyes clouded with tears. I closed them and leaned against the wall, pressing my sweaty cheek against the cool tiles. Breathing became difficult, and we were both coughing. I saw Muhammad wipe his eyes on his sleeve, smearing ash across one cheek. His face glistened with moisture—a mixture of sweat and tears from smoke. The pile of papers didn't look any smaller.

"My arms ache. Isn't this what they make prisoners do as torture?"

"Not exactly. You're not hanging by your arms."

I looked at his face, red from the heat of the fire, and his eyes red from the smoke. Why was I complaining? People were being shot and killed—I was merely hot and uncomfortable. Minutes passed like hours, punctuated by coughing.

"Damn it! I'm done." His anger startled me.

"What about the rest of the papers? We can't leave them here."

"We'll stuff them in the books."

"But if they find them, they'll think they're yours." He answered with a grunt as he worked to smother the small flames in the bucket. "But you said—"

"I'll be fine. We just got here, remember?" He had already gathered the papers and headed out of the room with me trailing behind.

The side wall of "our" bedroom had stacks of squarish packages wrapped in brown grocery bags and tied with twine, all the books we knew would be difficult to replace. Muhammad had been collecting history and political science books since graduate school. I added my own collection and some favorite children's books—all in packages weighing five kilograms, or eleven pounds. Jordan's postal regulations limited the weight of each package, but shipping books by post was far cheaper than any other method. Customs officials had ripped open random packages, apparently doubtful than anyone wanted that many books. Muhammad was taking a few papers at a time and jamming them into the open packages when a niece ran into the room.

"They're next door. Mama hung Father's dress uniform on the front door. She'll try to talk them out of coming inside."

I grabbed a few papers and tried to force them into a tightly bound package with ripped paper. I knew how strong the twine was because I'd wrapped each and every one of them, weighing them on a borrowed bathroom scale. Before I had the pages totally hidden, I heard voices at the door. Muhammad shoved the few remaining pages elbow deep between packages. Then he grabbed the one I was still poking and flipped it so the open end faced inward.

The bedroom door opened. Two soldiers pushed their way into the room, nearly tripping over our children who squeezed past them to get to us. The children had no idea what was happening, but they grabbed my legs as Muhammad spoke to the soldiers. I didn't understand what he was saying, but his voice was calm and steady. I pulled the boys close.

The soldiers looked around the room. One of them gestured to the stacks of book packages. I didn't need to understand the words to follow the conversation.

"What's that?"

"Books."

"All that's books?"

"Yes. All books."

"Why?"

The soldier walked over and pulled back a couple of torn wrappers. My heart pounded so hard I was sure he could hear it. The torn wrappers revealed books. Only books. He chose two closed packages at random and tore into them. More books. He whacked a package or two. Nothing squishy; nothing rattled. Books are solid.

He saw the two suitcases on the floor and gestured to the other soldier to open them. He poked around with the barrel of his rifle. I was thankful he didn't have a bayonet. Something rattled. He gestured for the other soldier to look and see what it was. The younger soldier stood up with a brown stick in his hand. He grasped it by both ends, and it looked to me as though he was going to break it in half.

"No!" It slipped out before I could stop it. Both men turned to look at me. "They're toys. Toys for my children." I knew they didn't speak English. I waved my hands and pointed to the boys still clinging to me. I reached for the Lincoln Log. "It's just a toy." Muhammad must have translated because the soldier surrendered the stick. I heard

59

the word "America" a few times. The soldiers moved on to the other rooms. My husband went with them.

I pulled the boys toward the big bed. I hadn't realized how tense and frightened I'd been until the soldiers left the room. My knees felt weak as I coaxed Ibrahim and Faisal onto the bed for a story. I needed to be with my children in that room, which, now that the soldiers had left, felt safe and welcoming.

The front bedroom was ours for as long as we wanted to stay, or as long as things remained calm in the neighborhood. If fighting broke out again, I knew Um Yusef would roust us out as she had the first time, saying, "I didn't wait all these years for you to come home just so you could get killed in my bed. Now get up and go into the back room to be safe." We did, and that's how the four of us ended up in a single bed while a dispossessed niece crowded in with one of her sisters.

Now things were calm, except for the searching house-to-house. Calm wasn't the same as normal.

Each morning a different section of the town woke to find themselves under virtual house arrest. The streets were closed, and soldiers stood on every corner to make sure everyone stayed in place.

"What were they looking for?" I asked later that night as I snuggled in close so our voices wouldn't wake the little ones sleeping on pallets on the floor next to us.

"Who knows? Guns, papers like the ones we burned, or memorabilia showing sympathy with the fighters, badges, pictures, maps...anything that might indicate disloyalty to the king." He stopped talking and played with a stray lock of my hair. "I think they were just making a big show to make sure each and every person understood who won the battle, who was in charge, and who was not welcome. I heard that young men are being arrested and held for just having the wrong accent."

"You can tell Palestinians by their accent?"

"This is a civil war. Think about your own civil war. Don't you think you could tell the Union soldiers from the Confederates by their accent?"

"Sometimes. Not always. The American Civil War split a lot of families. Sometimes brothers enlisted on opposite sides."

"Same thing here."

"Not really. A lot of these young men weren't even born in 1948. They were born here, in Jordan, and lived here all their lives. How can they have a distinct accent?"

"You'll see. The main social circle is the extended family, and friends of the family. Traditionally, they all came from the same village. When they left, they found safety in being close to the friends that were familiar to them. That's why today there are Palestinian neighborhoods and Jordanian neighborhoods. Hashemi Shemali is Palestinian, and a lot of them are from Qalqiliya and the surrounding villages. When people left their villages, they traveled together for protection. They settled together. Even in the camps, people from the same village cluster together. People keep the accents of their families."

"So, does that mean—"

"It means go to sleep. It's been a long day. If we oversleep, they'll eat all the labneh before we get up, and there won't be any left for us."

"Mmmmm. Can't let that happen." Even in the dark with my eyes closed, I could see his smile.

LABNEH, THE UNSUNG HERO

Labneh was created thousands of years ago and adapted to the nomadic lifestyle of the Bedouins. A dried version, only used in cooking, looks like rocks and has to be soaked overnight before using, but it travels well, takes little space, and lasts virtually forever.[1]

The form of labneh that Um Yusef served us resembled cream cheese in appearance and texture. The form that is sold in specialty stores in the United States is much softer, resembling a thicker than normal Greek yogurt. It has a much shorter shelf life and must be refrigerated. The advantage to the denser form is that it can be preserved in olive oil and does not need refrigeration.

Jam-packed with protein and calcium, the slightly salty food is also a probiotic. Probiotics keep the intestinal micro biome healthy, aiding digestion and boosting the immune system. Labneh also has less lactose and sugar than regular yogurt.[2, 3, 4] How can all that goodness also be so delicious?

References for history and nutritional information:
[1] bit.ly / PalLabneh1
[2] bit.ly / PalLabneh2
[3] bit.ly / PalLabne3
[4] bit.ly / PalLabneh4

TRY IT YOURSELF

One of the great things about labneh is how easy it is to make. Although all the recipes online and elsewhere talk about cheese cloth and raw milk or yogurt starters, I make mine the easy way. Several of the websites mentioned above have recipes and directions. Some start with homemade yogurt, others with a mixture of Greek yogurt and milk. My method strips it down to the basic essentials.

I buy a large container of plain yogurt from the grocery store, preferably one that says it has active cultures. Then line a small colander or a large strainer with two or three layers of sturdy paper towels that extend beyond the edges so they can wrap the yogurt. A friend of mine uses coffee filters.

Dump the yogurt into the colander or strainer and wrap the paper towels around it so no yogurt escapes when you apply pressure. Place a small dish on top and weigh it down with something heavy, such as a jar or can of food. This will squeeze water out of the yogurt. It can take 24 to 48 hours to get the consistency you want.

If you want to keep it refrigerated and use as a dip, 24 hours should be enough. Soft labneh should always be refrigerated and consumed within a few days. The softer form of labneh is usually plated with olive oil drizzled on the top. Toppings add visual interest and taste. Paprika, sumac, chopped nuts, mint and cucumbers—the possibilities are endless. I've even seen it mixed with green avocado.

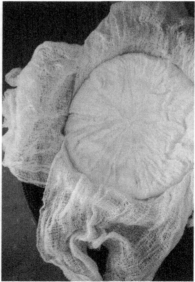

Both photos by Amelia Crook via Wylio.com

Photo of soft labneh with zaatar by Jessica Spengler via flickr

If you want to make it into balls and preserve them in olive oil, you will need to wait until it is thick enough to roll between your hands and keep its shape. The drier it is, the longer it lasts. Be sure to coat your hands with olive oil while forming the balls, or the labneh will stick to your hands. Also, if the balls are not completely covered in oil, they can go bad. Even a small spot of one ball sticking above the top of the olive oil can begin to grow a slimy mold that, left unattended, can grow down through the oil and spoil more than a single ball.

When the labneh has reached the desired consistency, add salt to taste, mixing it thoroughly. If you have a recipe or know how much salt to use, you can add the salt at the beginning when it mixes more easily. The only reason I add the salt at the end, is that I gauge the amount of salt by taste, and I can't taste it properly while it's still yogurt.

Although it is almost always served as a savory item, I love putting it in a sandwich with jam or jelly.

Photo by Petra via flickr.com

Soft versions appear on veggie plates or mixed with other flavors with chips. The possibilities are endless.

_____

Similar recipe: [5] bit.ly / PalLabneh5

Photo by Amelia Crook via Wylio.com

Canned Cheese and Fresh Tomatoes

Eventually, the radio announcer's statement came true. Law and order, or at least quiet was restored in Zarqa. People began to venture out to check on their neighbors or to see if the corner shop had any cigarettes. I had no clear idea of time passing.

Maybe it was a week. Maybe two weeks, but one day Muhammad said he'd heard that cars were running to Amman, and he was going to see what he could do about getting a job.

"How do you find a job? Is there a classified section in the paper?"

"You talk to people. People know people and pass you on to someone else who might know more. We can use any job right now. Once life gets back to normal, I can look for something else."

"When will you be back."

"No telling. I hope to be back tonight, but if things get difficult, I'll stay at my sister's or my uncle's. Don't worry if I'm not back tonight. There are still skirmishes in Amman and you know how transportation disappears at the first sound of gun shots."

That was not reassuring. "I thought the fighting was all over. Did all the fighters just move to another place?"

"Not exactly. Some neighborhoods are stronger than others." I didn't understand what that meant, but he was antsy to be on his way, so I'd wished him luck.

He left right after breakfast, and we all waited. Was I the only one worried? Was I the only one who wouldn't sleep if he didn't get home? I couldn't ask. I had already figured out that one did not discuss such worries out loud.

It was late afternoon when the doorbell rang. We all jumped, and conversations stopped mid-syllable. I scrambled to my feet and went to press my nose to the bedroom window that looked out onto the courtyard. Was it Muhammad? Faisal tugged on my clothes, and I lifted him up to watch Feryal unlock the iron door from the courtyard to the street.

"Baba!" Faisal squirmed out of my arms and ran to the door with me in his wake. I smothered a giggle as everyone in the house clustered in the entryway. It made me think of puppies running at the sound of the can opener. Guess we'd been cooped up a little too long.

Muhammad barely had room to close the house door as the family clustered around for news. His eyes moved from one to the other as the questions flew at him like machine gun fire.

"What's it like out there?"

"Are the cars running?"

"Of course the cars are running, or he wouldn't have been gone all day."

"Did you see the family on Hashemi?"

"Is everyone all right?"

"Is the market open?"

"Can we go buy food?"

"The water truck came today."

"Are things quiet in Amman?"

I didn't ask my question because I could tell by the set of his shoulders that the answer would be negative. He held up his hand, and gradually the voices stopped. "If somebody brings me a glass of tea, I'll answer all your questions."

I surprised myself with how well I followed the barrage.

Not only did I know the words but also the meaning behind the words. When they asked about the cars, they were not talking about cars in general but the service cabs. And they were asking if the roads were open and the soldiers were allowing civilians to travel freely. We had all been housebound for days, and the nieces had little to do, so I'd had nonstop Arabic lessons. Apparently, their efforts were making a difference.

The fighting in our neighborhood had stopped, but we still felt under siege. Muhammad's brother, Abu Yusef, had not been home since the fighting started. Like many Palestinian officers in the Jordanian Army, he was under investigation. The uncertainty about his well-being was a cloud hanging over everyone in the house. The army suspended his pay during the investigation.

How could Muhammad hope to find a job amidst all the chaos? Muhammad and I both knew that we were an additional burden on the already strained resources of the family. The municipal water was not yet running, so still no showers, but somehow, he'd left the house this morning looking (and smelling) fresh and hopeful.

I was almost weak with relief that he was home, even though he'd told me I shouldn't worry. Now he was back, and I felt as though I'd been holding my breath all day.

We all trooped into the living room and settled into the "company" chairs. A huge tray with a teakettle and glasses for everyone appeared like magic. Um Yusef poured me a glass before adding the sugar to the kettle and pouring glasses for everyone else. Once again, I made things more difficult. I took my boys' glasses into the kitchen and added powdered milk before bringing them back. It delighted me when the two youngest cousins brought their glasses into the kitchen for me to add milk to them as well.

I hurried back to hear the report of Muhammad's adventures.

69

* * *

"First, the main street of the market is almost an inch deep in broken glass. Not a single window remains intact. Some upstairs windows have blackened edges, so they must have had a direct hit. I think the entire downtown area would have been flattened if the buildings weren't solid stone.

"A few army jeeps are crunching their way through the glass, but the main street is closed to ordinary traffic, and most of the soldiers are on foot patrol. Lots of soldiers. As you guessed, once you get to the station, cars are running. The drivers need the money." He gave a quick laugh. A lot of people needed money now, including us. "I was lucky enough to get a car with a talkative driver. He said there's still heavy fighting in some areas around the refugee camps. The army claims to have 'restored law and order' throughout the country, and it's largely true, but pockets of resistance are using the urban guerrilla tactics of hit and run."

"What about Hashemi?" Again, I knew what they meant—Jebel Al-Hashimi or Hashemi Al-Shemali, one of the mountains on which Amman was built. In 1948, when the refugees from the formation of the state of Israel arrived, Hashemi was so far outside of the city that land was cheap. Palestinians lucky enough to have a little money in their pockets when they fled bought land and settled there. The members of our family that lived in Amman lived there.

"Our family is safe."

"Thank God." The low-voiced comment came from several people around the room. I almost laughed when Ibrahim, our five-year-old, came in at the tail end. Did he know what he was saying and why? Probably. His Arabic was moving a lot faster than mine, even without people trying to teach him.

"I was a little worried about getting a car willing to go to a place as heavily populated by Palestinians as Hashemi, but there was no need. They did see a lot of action, but it seems as quiet as our neighborhood now, at least in the daytime." He took a sip of his tea. "Speaking of our neighborhood, what's a water truck?"

All the girls started explaining at once. Not for the first time, I marveled at the speed with which the babble subsided, and a spokesperson emerged. It was Feryal, the fourth daughter who told the tale.

"The army sent one of their tanker trucks to give out water to civilians. The soldier opened the tap and people stood in line with jerrycans and buckets. We were lucky because it stopped right in front of our house, so we got to fill up twice before it moved on."

"Can't you smell the difference?" I added in English, only half joking. "We heated water, and everyone managed a good sponge bath. There is nothing better than pouring a can of hot water over yourself after so many days. It was an amazing morale boost." It was a new experience for me to scoop some near-boiling water from a washtub balanced atop a kerosene burner into a plastic basin of unheated tap water. Then I stood near the floor drain and washed. I managed to get the boys and myself reasonably clean with minimal water use. I didn't add that using the same towel when it was my turn was not as pleasant. No one knew when water would run again, and I don't think the entire family used as much water as a single shower would have used back home. No, I corrected myself. This was home now. I had to stop thinking of the States as "back home."

"Has something happened to the tank?" Muhammad looked to Um Yusef for the answer.

"No, but even so, the water level was getting low. We emptied the water into the tank as fast as we could, and it helped. I feel sorry for people with no storage tanks."

Another niece gathered the empty tea glasses, and the little ones decided the excitement was over and escaped. When only the adults and near-adults were in the room, Um Yusef's face got serious. "You said they saw a lot of action. I

71

guess that means a lot of street fighting." At Muhammad's nod, she continued. "How's your car?"

Our car! I felt like someone had thrown me into a freezing pool. My breath stopped; my stomach lurched; I felt numb all over. How could I forget the car? That was our life's savings! It wasn't merely a car—it was our small business. We expected it to support us if necessary, or provide extra income for furniture, rent for a place to live, any of the many things we would need to set up housekeeping in another country. We were starting with nothing.

Shortly after our arrival in July, a relative had come to us with the news of a low mileage, late model Mercedes 190 that had just arrived from Germany. The man who brought it had a family crisis and wanted to sell it right away, and he was only asking what he'd paid for it. As the men talked, they developed a business plan. Not exactly on the back of a napkin, but the same general idea.

We would convert the car into a private taxi. First, we'd remove the two front seats and replace them with one long seat to accommodate one extra person in front. The cousin knew a man who did that kind of work. He also knew a man who knew another man willing to sell (or rent) a set of green license plates. In an effort to control the traffic congestion, the government limited the number of the green license plates that denote a car for hire. The going rate to buy plates from the owner was the equivalent of a year's salary. We elected to rent them. That payment was merely for the privilege of putting them on our car. We still had to pay the steep government fee to actually use them.

The cousin with the plan and all the connections was an experienced driver. He would drive the car, collect the money from the passengers, pay for gas, license plate rental, and his daily salary, and bring us the remainder at the end of each week.

It had sounded like a great idea, and it should have been, but I couldn't help thinking of that snippet of poetry by Robert Burns about the "best laid plans of mice and men" as I looked at Muhammad's face. Even in the brief period it had been in service, the car had not earned its keep. The cousin, like all the other drivers, would high-tail it home at the first sound of gunfire. He'd park the car out of sight of the road in the space between his father's house and Muhammad's sister's house, giving it as much protection as he could.

The look on my husband's face said something serious had happened.

"Our car deserves a purple heart." He was switching from Arabic to English and back as he spoke. He wanted to make sure I, too, understood. The discussion about family had been in Arabic with me catching words and phrases and making assumptions. He would fill in the blanks later. This, however, was my need-to-know area. I processed the remark while he explained to the others a purple heart was an honor given to U.S. soldiers killed or wounded in active combat.

"Is she dead?"

"She is a heroine! No, she is not dead, but could be in critical condition. Don't worry, cars never die in this country. Look at Khalil's Volvo. It's older than you are and still in running condition." I smiled at him, because I knew that was what he wanted.

"What makes her a heroine?"

"Remember that I said they saw a lot of action? Well, it took longer to subdue Hashemi than Zarqa. Government forces fought their way up the mountain street by street." I could picture it. The houses were close together, and the neighborhoods were all Palestinian. Muhammad had explained one day as we went up the winding road leading to his sister and uncle's houses, that each little neighborhood was settled mainly by people from one area. People from Qalqilya, his hometown settled the top of the mountain. Once the soldiers had fought their way to the top, where could the street fighters go? They probably had paths between houses where they could disappear. But women, children, and non-combatants occupied all of those close-packed houses.

"Eyes were peeking from every window when the fighters retreated. Three of the commandos ducked behind my sister's house, but the soldiers were right behind them. The fighters dove under the car. The soldiers fired their automatics...and kept firing. Everyone was convinced the fighters were dead. The women were crying. The soldiers moved on...and...the three fighters rolled out from under the car and disappeared between the houses on their way down the mountain."

In a low voice, meant only for me, he asked, "If you could have spent the money to save the lives of three good men, wouldn't you have done it?"

My eyes stung with unshed tears. "Yes, of course."

His arm went around my shoulders, then he turned back to the others. "The car needs five new tires, and they shot out every single window. We aren't sure about the engine, but it looks intact."

"Five tires?"

"Yeah, they even got the spare."

"It must have a lot of bullet holes."

"To be honest, it looks like a sieve."

"But you don't think it's dead?"

"Nope, and neither are the three fighters. Bullet holes in cars are easy to fix."

* * *

The next morning, we woke up to the sound of a man's voice outside our bedroom door. It sounded as though he was arguing with Um Yusef. Muhammad got up and stuck his head out into the hallway, then he went out and closed the door behind him. I could hear his voice, calm and reasonable. My language skills were still too weak to

74

translate anything that filtered through a solid door.

At last, I heard the clang of the iron front door. When Muhammad finally came back, he was laughing.

"What's so funny?"

"Um Yusef very diplomatically told me to leave her alone to do what she does."

"Which is…"

"She just went to the UNRWA distribution site and got a sack of flour. She hired a man with a handcart to bring it to the house. He said he never agreed to carry it inside for the price she wanted to pay. I solved it by paying him a little extra for carrying the fifty-pound sack inside and putting it where she wanted it."

"So, what's the problem?"

He laughed again. "She said he would have been happy with half as much, and she would have paid him that if I had stayed out of it. Apparently, there's a ritual. He has to ask for more, and she has to say it was included. Then they compromise, and they both feel like winners. She knew exactly how much she was going to pay before she left the house today."

"She did all that before we woke up?"

"She says if she doesn't get there to stand in line before they open, there won't be anything left. And she needs the flour."

"Can't argue with that." My attention switched as the boys stirred. Ibrahim sat up with the hair at the crown of his head sticking up like a rooster's comb. Faisal kicked off his covers and smiled at me. The angelic look probably meant his bed was wet. With the shortage of water, we'd been spreading his mattress and bedding on the roof each day, letting it air and dry in the blistering September sun. He didn't seem to mind, and there wasn't a lot we could do about it if he did.

We were just about finished getting ready to face the day, when the doorbell rang. "Man! These people do more before the sun gets up than most people do all day." I was exaggerating but this wasn't the first time we'd had guests arrive with the sun.

The first few weeks we'd been here, there had been a constant stream of people coming to welcome Muhammad home and gawk at his foreign family. No, that's unfair. Most of them were very nice and scolded the children who gawked. It was disconcerting to wake up with company in the living room. I'd sit and smile until my cheeks hurt. I couldn't understand anything more than an occasional word. One silver lining to Black September—no one had come visiting until now.

Um Yusef stopped me on the way to the bathroom to introduce me to her brother. "And look what he brought us!" She pulled me to the kitchen door and pointed to a box of the most beautiful vine-ripened tomatoes I'd ever seen. My mouth watered just looking at them. We hadn't had fresh fruits or vegetables in days. I'd stopped counting, but it must have been two weeks or more. Things were looking up.

The brother kissed Um Yusef on both cheeks, shook Muhammad's hand, and waved at me as he hurried out the door. "He has to get home to bring food to his wives and children," Muhammad explained.

"His wives?"

"It's a long story. Maybe Um Yusef will tell you about him later." His whole face lit up with a grin. "Hey, why don't you and the kids come with me today? We can go to Hashemi and have something other than these four walls to look at for a change. I'll drop you off at my sister's and run down a couple of leads on jobs. When I'm done, I'll come back and visit for a few hours before we come back here."

The idea of seeing the outside again made my heart beat faster. All other thoughts left my mind as I corralled the boys into a quick breakfast and searched for shoes they hadn't worn since the fighting started. I grabbed a labneh sandwich and asked permission to eat a tomato. Um Yusef laughed as

I bit into the red ripe fruit with what must have been an expression of bliss. "It's not an apple, you know."

"It's even better than an apple." I intended to add something about vitamins but stopped talking to keep the juice from dribbling down my chin. It was much better than any apple I could remember.

We were out the door in record time. I wasn't the only one excited to be outdoors. Muhammad soon decided it was easier to carry Faisal than to chase the two-year-old or wait for him to investigate every little shiny thing along the way. We turned onto the main street that led to the bus and taxi station. Our high spirits became somber before we went very far.

Rubble often blocked the sidewalks. Fire had gutted many stores. Some upper-story windows were missing, along with parts of the surrounding structure. Black gaping holes showed the aftermath of fires. We were walking down the middle of the street, and our footsteps crunched through broken glass and spent bullet casings. Ibrahim kept busy filling his pockets with the bullet casings. Between piles of rubble, broken doors, bent metal shelving and other detritus of the conflict, merchants had piles and pyramids of goods for sale. "I'm amazed anyone has anything to sell."

"If this had happened in the States, there'd be nothing left but dust and toothpicks," said Muhammad. "Most of these buildings are solid stone. It takes a direct hit to make a dent. Some of the upper stories are cement block if the owners can't afford the stone."

"Are these the men who own the shops?"

"Maybe some of them are, but others just find a space and do what they can to put food on the table." We stopped at a pyramid of shiny greenish cans. "Cheese," said Muhammad. He bought two cans and gave them to me to carry. He put Faisal down while he paid the man. I looked at the cans and saw a familiar symbol of clasped hands. This was aid from the United States! It said NOT FOR SALE in huge letters, yet here we were, buying it.

I pointed to the print on the can. "How does that happen?" My outrage flamed. This was supposed to be free for people in need. Muhammad just shrugged. As we moved away, he talked in a low voice.

"Think about it. The aid has to have a distribution channel. It's a matter of corruption in the distribution channel, probably fairly high in the government. Someone is lining his pockets." This only made my outrage worse. He continued, "It could have been worse. This way, we get to buy cheese, the guy that sold it to us puts food on his table, and it gets distributed more widely than if it disappeared to friends and family of the government official. Only the United Nations has a distribution channel in place because they've been helping the refugees for decades. That's where we get the flour for our daily bread." He reminded me of the sack of flour Um Yusef brought home that morning. I decided to save my outrage for something more meaningful. Yes, someone who didn't need it was benefitting, but so were we and many others.

We finally reached the station, and Muhammad led us past the regular taxis, an unthinkable luxury in our current unemployed status. Instead, we walked on a few more yards to the service (pronounced "serveece") cars going to downtown Amman. These private licensed taxis, almost always Mercedes like our own car, often had a set route and acted like small buses, not moving until passengers filled all seats and charging a set price per seat. We filled the back seat and waited for two more passengers to sit in front. Everyone would get out at the destination and go their separate ways. We would walk to another service stop and get a car that went from downtown to Hashemi.

The ride to Amman was quiet. I was getting used to armed soldiers on every street corner. Other than that, there was very little sign of disruption. It was as though once we left the main street of Zarqa, a blanket of normalcy had been thrown over the country. It was a weird feeling, knowing that violence on a scale I could not have imagined outside of a movie screen had been going on for days—yet today we were on a normal family outing to visit relatives.

CHEESE FOR BREAKFAST

Typical Arab breakfasts are collections of foods that vary from family to family, from region to region, and from one situation to another. We often invited people for breakfast, and the more people we expected, the more variety we served. One important part of our breakfast was, and still is, cheese. This includes different types of cheese, many of which are imported, but are common enough to be considered part of an ordinary breakfast.

White cheese may have a proper name, but I have no recollection of hearing it referred to as anything other than white cheese. This soft, white cheese is only available in the spring when fresh milk is plentiful. Made from ewe or goat milk, it is usually heavily salted to prevent spoilage. In addition to being a nutritious and delicious breakfast dish, this soft cheese can also be soaked overnight to remove the salt for use in desserts. It is featured in many delicious desserts such as *knafeh* and *qatayef*, and recipes for these dishes that appear on the internet often substitute ricotta cheese, but ricotta is much softer than white cheese. The Palestinian town of Nablus is famous for the desserts and the eponymous *nabulsi* cheese.

Nabulsi cheese is a salty, white, boiled cheese formed into squares two to three inches on a side and less than an inch thick. Salt is added throughout the process of making the milk into cheese. The salt draws out the whey, and by the end of the process the cheese is quite hard and very salty. It is then covered in brine. Most households buy it in five-gallon tins. The squares of cheese thus preserved in brine will last for months without spoiling. The cheese never lasted that long in our house because everyone, especially Faisal, loved to eat it at any time of day.

When served for breakfast, nabulsi cheese can be soaked for several hours or overnight to lower the salt content before serving. It can also be fried in hot oil until golden brown outside and stretchy and chewy inside. Be sure to pat the cheese dry before placing it in hot oil, and never start with a cold pan as the cheese will melt into a gooey mess before turning golden.

If you're feeling adventurous, try making your own cheese. I did it a few times, and the results were delicious. My cheese was soft and not meant for long term storage, but both options are possible at home. Again, instructions are easy to find. I have no secret shortcuts for this. Just pay attention and get the temperature of the milk right.[1]

Kashkaval - A common imported cheese, kashkaval can be made from either sheep or cow milk. It is often made in Bulgaria and is sold in small wheels about six inches in diameter and about two inches thick. It is an off-white color and similar to cheddar in texture, but a bit harder. Even though it is not made in Palestine, it is common enough that it has become part of the normal diet. Muhammad had fond memories of eating kashkaval as a child.

Cheddar - Although I'm sure things have changed in the last few decades, at the time of this story cheddar cheese was only bought in cans, usually distinctively blue cans about the size and shape of tuna cans and was a Kraft product. In fact, the mild cheddar cheese was referred to colloquially as "Kraft cheese." The cans we bought from the street vendor in this story were much larger, approximately quart size and army green in color, but the cheese was very similar—a pale yellow-orange mild cheddar.

80

Lebaneh or Labneh - As I mentioned in the last chapter, labneh is thickened yogurt drained of the whey. I only include labneh in this list because it is sold as a cheese in this country, but my relatives would not ordinarily include it in a list of cheeses.

_____

(1) bit.ly / PalCheese1

FRESH TOMATOES

Breakfast is one area that brought out cultural differences most sharply. I found it startling how many illogical yet deeply rooted ideas I had. The very idea of eating vegetables at breakfast made me laugh. I grew up with a limited choice of fruit being suitable choices for breakfast. Orange or grapefruit juice, a cut half of grapefruit were common, or perhaps a banana sliced into cereal. On special occasions cantaloupe or honeydew might be served, or strawberries on pancakes. Vegetables never made an appearance at breakfast. I'm not sure how much this was just my family or how much was the cultural norm, but I saw nothing on breakfast tables in movies or on television to make me think my family was unusual in that respect.

An Arab breakfast is much more inclusive. The fruit served at breakfast expands to include whatever fruit is available in the market. Perhaps even more common than fruit at breakfast, cut fresh veggies appear on the breakfast table. Fresh tomatoes cut in wedges can have their own plate or add color to the cheese plates, as do spears of small cucumbers, and occasionally green onions. These vegetables go particularly well with most of the breakfast foods. Olives, another startling addition to breakfast, soon became a staple.

Over the years, we developed our own brand of breakfast, one that combined elements of both cultures.

Photo by Quinn Dabrowski via wylio   Photo by stu_spivak via wylio.com

Photo by Andrew Malone via wylio   Photo by David J. via wylio.com

Photo by Kandukuru Nagarjun via wylio.com

Pickles for Breakfast?

The Hashemi service cab let us out a few yards from Zahara's (a.k.a. Um Abdullah's) front gate. All four of us were greeted like long-lost relatives when we stepped into Um Abdullah's house. In a way, that's what we were. With no communication between the family in Amman and the family in Zarqa, anything could have happened, and we all had worries over what may have happened to those we could not see. Fighting had been heavy, and we'd seen ample evidence that many private residences had been hit and hit hard. The miracle was that we all survived without a scratch. If the only casualty in the Hallaj family was our car, we accepted it gratefully. Many families were not that lucky. Later reports varied wildly. The Jordanians claimed 3,400 Palestinians were killed, but the Palestinians gave estimates at over 10,000. Everyone seemed to agree that most of the casualties were civilians.

After we got our breath back from the bear hugs, Um Abdullah pulled me into the living room and Muhammad and the boys followed. Not letting go of my hand, she sat next to me and began her eye-witness account of the events of the last few days. I guess the rest of the extended family was as tired of being stuck within their own four walls as we were because other familiar faces came in and joined us. Since Muhammad had heard her story the day before, she directed her words to me. The facts matched what Muhammad had told us about how our car earned its purple heart, but today's telling was more vivid and immediate. Tapping a recent memory, the emotions were raw and came

83

through with the words. New arrivals to the room raised their voices above hers, adding details seen from the vantage points at other windows. Voices built up in ever-louder layers leading to a climax whose volume must have rivaled the machine guns. Each speaker accompanied his or her words with exaggerated gestures and hand waving, possibly as a supplement for my meager vocabulary, but it increased the atmosphere of chaos.

"The officer shouted, 'Enough!'" Um Abdullah's hand went up, palm out, mimicking the officer's gesture. "And the guns stopped." The competing voices in the room quieted. "'This will be the last service cab they ever ride,' he said, and he laughed." Um Abdallah shuddered. Even though we all knew the final outcome, I heard the quiver of tears close to the surface of Um Abdullah's voice as she described her feelings as the soldiers walked away, satisfied they had done their duty.

By the time the ubiquitous tea arrived, the story concluded with the fighters "rising from the dead" and scurrying down the hill to blend with the civilian population. There was a general shifting of positions after the tension of reliving the story. Some people took their tea and moved into the entry hall to sit on mats and have their own conversations. Abdullah, Zahara's oldest son, joined us. Muhammad immediately included him in the conversation. "If the fighters ducked under the car, why do you think the soldiers shot out the windows?"

"I don't know." Abdullah's shrug and flat voice added that he didn't care either. "I wasn't showing my face in the window." He took a long drag on his cigarette. "If the soldiers caught me watching, they would have been the last thing I ever saw."

That didn't make sense to me, and I couldn't stop myself. "Why?"

"Because they'd think I was one of the fighters who just ducked into the house."

84

I heard a low snort of disbelief from someone on my side of the room.

"I know why." The statement came from Muhammad's uncle. I'd thought he was dozing in his chair, so I was surprised to hear him speak up.

"Why what?" Muhammad was lost. At least it wasn't just me.

"Why they shot the windows and the seats, of course. Wasn't that what you asked?" His raspy old voice barely carried across the room.

"Yes." Muhammad moved to his uncle's side and the conversation continued in a near whisper.

"The first soldier who came around the house shouted that they were trying to start the car and drive away."

"He didn't see them slide under it?"

Uncle Abu Khalil shrugged. "Maybe. Maybe not." His face crinkled in a mischievous grin. "Your brother isn't the only Palestinian in the Jordanian army."

"You knew that, and you let your wife and the others cry over the guerrilla fighters?" Muhammad asked.

"Women talk too much."

I was gratified that he apparently considered me an exception. I took a breath to acknowledge the fact, but at Muhammad's frown, I looked away as though I hadn't heard a word they'd said. On second thought, he probably thought I didn't understand his words. On the contrary, I not only understood his words but the implication behind them. Abu Khalil was holding up his end of a daisy chain of trust.

"Then they came to take me away." His voice, suddenly stronger, launched into his own adventure. "Of course, the *shebab* panicked. Young men don't need to show their faces these days." He gave a short laugh as his fingers spread representing the young men trying to scatter within the small house. "My wife went to the door. After all, no one shoots a hajji, right?"

"Only a madman." Muhammad answered with a

chuckle. The two men shared a silent joke about fierce old women.

"When the soldiers asked for the old man, she asked what the army wanted with an old man who couldn't hear and with bad knees, but the soldiers only said the officer in charge wanted me. I was worried they were going to grill me about what I saw from the window. What could I say? I'm guessing they saw me, or they wouldn't have known an old man lived in the house."

"Did you go with them?"

"What else could I do? They had the guns." Abu Khalil paused, and I imagined I saw emotions run across his face. Fear? Worry? Resignation? All questions I couldn't ask. "I expected questions and maybe to be knocked around if I didn't answer."

"And?" Muhammad prompted.

"The officer gave me a written message and said I had to find the fighters and deliver the message. Then he shooed me away with his hand and said, 'Go! Find the fighters.' So I went." He gave a little shudder. "As I walked away, I thought I could feel the spot on my back where the bullet would hit when they shot me." He took a sip of his tea. "I ducked out of their line of sight as soon as I could. I broke a twig off a little tree and tied my handkerchief to it as I walked. I turned into a sheltered alley as soon as I could and started shouting for the fighters—again expecting a bullet to stop my shouting—but it didn't. Instead, someone answered. I walked toward the voice, waving my little handkerchief, and finally a man appeared and took the message. I saw at least two others with their Kalashnikovs pointed in my direction. He told me to wait, and the other guys were right there to make sure I didn't move. That was a looooong wait."

Muhammad shook his head. "I bet those guns look a lot bigger when you're looking down the business end." Abu Khalil nodded.

"Finally, the first guy came back and told me I could go home. If I saw the officer again to tell him the message was received and agreed. Then he started shouting to the men that they had one hour to disappear. That army officer was gone when I got home, but that was the end of the shooting."

"That's amazing! You are a better negotiator than the guy from the United Nations! I've always known you were a hero, Uncle."

* * *

Lunch was a festive occasion with potato stew served over rice. Meat was conspicuous by its absence. The local butcher had nothing to sell. Neither did the greengrocer. Despite what the radio was saying, the country was by no means back to normal. After lunch, Muhammad went off to see a man about a job. We had no sooner cleared away the food when my father-in-law and his wife came to visit. They were sorry to have missed Muhammad but were delighted to see the children. We spread sitting mats around the central room of the house, and everyone sat on the floor, leaning on the walls or pillows.

Soon the children went outside to play with cousins living in Abu Khalil's house. I didn't worry about them; there were a hundred eyes looking at them. Everyone treated my children as though they were their own. This was good, because I didn't have to keep them within my sight at all times. I never feared for their safety. If they were doing something wrong, I heard about it quickly. I was generally happy about this surveillance, although there were times I was sorely tempted to gather my ducklings under my wings to protect them from what I thought were unreasonable expectations. I felt bad for Ibrahim. As an inquisitive five-year-old, he got the brunt of reprimands that confused him. He was used to a set of rules, and now the rules kept changing in ways he couldn't predict. Why, for example, had his grandfather sent him away from the dinner table when he was telling us about the worm he found? I still remember the hurt look on his face as he got up and left the table. Muhammad saw by my expression that I was about to defend my son and gave me a warning poke in the ribs. The boys and I learned the boundaries of polite conversation together. My corrections may have been less public but were no less embarrassing.

The afternoon settled into a calm quiet as Muhammad's father invited me to play *mahbooseh*, a form of backgammon. He had been a frequent visitor to Zarqa in the unsettled weeks leading up to open hostilities, and I had missed our games, even though I lost consistently. He enjoyed teaching me the intricacies of the game, pointing out my mistakes and waiting for me to make a better choice of moves. The murmur of two or three conversations were a pleasant buzz in the background. We were just starting our second game when a single roll of the dice changed my strong position to one of complete hopelessness. He caught one of my pieces very near the starting position, meaning there was no way at all to avoid being trounced.

My mind wandered away from the board and I compared the game with our present position. We had arrived with what I thought of as a healthy bank account to start our new life. We'd invested a sizeable chunk of that money into a small business—buying a car that would bring in a small but steady income. We weren't broke, and our situation was far from hopeless, but if something didn't change soon, where were we headed? I had no idea how much the repairs on the car would be, and I had even less of an idea how much it would take for us to live. I was still at the stage where I converted prices into dollars and cents and tried to make decisions based on my knowledge of prices in the States, a very different economy. I knew we wouldn't go hungry. After all, family helped family, but I'd rather be in the position of one who helped rather than always being the one who needed help.

I looked around the room. Muhammad's brother-in-law was sitting talking about nothing in particular with a couple of cousins. Ordinarily they would be working, not sitting around drinking tea and smoking increasingly hard-to-get cigarettes. Khalil, the brother-in-law, drove a truck to and from Saudi Arabia, Iraq and other Arab countries, as did his brothers, Saadu and Faiz. Now there was nothing to transport. No goods had come into Jordan for weeks. It wasn't just meat and vegetables that were disappearing from the market, so were cigarettes, sugar, matches, soap, and countless other imports.

With Abu Yousef's pay suspended, the cousins who drove for a living out of work, and Muhammad still unemployed, what would the family live on if this situation continued? Family may help family, but the combined resources could only stretch so far. Muhammad's sister sewed dresses to earn money, but I was pretty sure no one was ordering new dresses now.

"Play." The command jerked me out of my daydreaming. I looked down at the board and saw that he could win in the next two turns. However, if I rolled a double six or a double five, I still had a chance of changing a two-point loss to a one-point loss—a hope that kept me from conceding earlier. I gave the dice a few extra shakes, closed my eyes, and threw them toward the board. A small chuckle from my father-in-law confirmed my fears. I opened my eyes to see the lowest score possible—a one and a two. I had to laugh.

The arrival of a car and the sound of Muhammad's voice cut short the expected laughter at my humiliating loss. The cousins were always asking why I played against him, the undisputed master of the game. My reply was always the same, "Why learn the game from a second-class player when I can learn from the master?"

Muhammad came in with a smile on his face. My heart jumped with excitement. It must mean he has a job! He gave me a half wave as he went directly to his father and greeted him first. The respect Muhammad showed for his father always impressed me. Far from feeling slighted, I was proud of him—and it was a wonderful example for our children. I closed the backgammon board, and Muhammad squeezed into the space between his father and me.

"Do you have everything you need, Father? Do you have enough water? Food? Cigarettes?"

I started to get up and make more room, but Muhammad's arm reached over and rested on my knee. I stayed.

Before that conversation was over, more people arrived. The cousins Saadu and Faiz came along with their wives. Next came Muhammad's aunt and uncle from the house behind us, and Jamal, the driver of our car. Two more cousins, whose names I didn't yet know, were met with some good-natured complaints about running out of room. Somehow, everyone found a place and Weedad, Zahara's teenage daughter, brought more mats until the room was wall-to-wall people. The noise level increased as the children came inside. Khalil switched on the porch light, and the young ones were told to play on the veranda. Um Abdullah came out of the kitchen with a large tray full of small tea glasses. Weedad followed on her heels with a huge tea kettle.

"You see how much trouble you cause?" Muhammad asked me in a voice meant to carry throughout the room.

"Me? I didn't ask for tea." The grin on his face said he was teasing, but I was still uncomfortable with what seemed like a hundred eyes all looking in my direction.

"No, but you do the unthinkable and drink tea without sugar. Now they have to make everyone's tea without sugar—all because of you."

Um Abdullah handed me the first glass. She laughed and shook her head. "Don't pay attention to him. It's no trouble." Meanwhile, I could see Weedad putting a small spoonful of sugar in each small glass and stirring them. The clink, clink of the spoon on each glass rang like a bell and added a festive atmosphere.

"It's almost seven o'clock." I couldn't tell who the timekeeper was, but suddenly all conversation stopped. I realized that the television was on with the sound muted. I hadn't even noticed. There was a rustle of movement as people shifted to face the TV. In the unaccustomed silence, the rattle of gunfire wiped their smiles off their faces. Children drifted in through the open door and found places in the crowded room.

"I hope we don't lose electricity again," said a female voice. "We haven't seen our show for three weeks."

Khalil pulled the curtains over the two small windows, turned off the lights, and closed the iron door. We sipped our tea in the flickering blue light of the television. The sound was still muted, and we could hear the automatic gunfire through the open windows. Apparently, we were all going to ignore it. I was all right with that, especially since there wasn't anything else we could do except worry. At least we didn't have a panicking schoolteacher in our midst.

Weedad resumed her work with the tea, but the spoon no longer sounded like bells. It was just an annoying clinking. "Did everyone get tea?" Her voice sounded unnaturally loud in the room. Someone spoke up on the other side of the room, and she poured another glass.

"We'll stay here tonight," Muhammad whispered in my ear. I didn't know if he meant just us, or everyone. Where would we all sleep?

"Quiet!" That was Afaf's voice, the oldest of Saleh's daughters. She was sitting right in front of the TV.

The screen lit up with the title of the show, Peyton Place. I nearly choked on my tea. They were all here to watch Peyton Place! I knew the show by reputation only. It had been wildly popular in the States a few years earlier. I knew the series was based on a book written by a couple who took turns writing in the attic. One would write while the other took care of cleaning up the supper things and getting the kids to bed. The next night they traded places. Each one had to read what the other had written before continuing the story. I had a vague notion the story line was about a small group of couples cheating on each other. It was considered a bit risqué, and I thought of it as a romance novel in soap opera clothing.

The show started, and Afaf read the subtitles. Then I understood why everyone had gathered. She was probably the only adult female who could read well enough to keep up with the subtitles! I was stunned to realize these capable, intelligent women might be semi-literate. I thought back on what Muhammad had told me about his family. His mother had died in childbirth when he was only four. He told me about his sister standing on a box to wash dishes and work in the kitchen. "Our sister took care of us," was the recollection of four-year-old Muhammad. "She couldn't go to school anymore because she had to take care of us. Saleh would come home from school and share his homework with Zahara. He taught her what he learned. When I got old enough for school, the three of us sat and did schoolwork. Saleh was our teacher."

I don't know how long they lived like that before their father married their mother's half-sister, believing that an aunt would take better care of the children than someone not related. I looked over at the woman they still called Aunt and remembered Muhammad saying, "We didn't want anyone else coming in and taking over our sister's place." The three children had drawn together with the death of their mother. I wondered how difficult that had been for her.

"Hush!" Afaf's scolding made me realize that the murmur of voices had been steadily escalating as the women tried to piece together what was happening after missing three weeks of episodes. The men appeared to be as engrossed as the women, but less vocal. If asked, I'm sure they would all have denied it.

At last the show was over, and I could talk. I got Muhammad's attention. "I can't stay the night. I don't have a toothbrush or anything."

"We can't get a car now. No one is on the streets."

Everyone started shuffling around with that restless mass movement that characterizes the end of a social evening. The cousins and their wives moved toward the door, answering my question of everyone staying. Apparently not. Each couple or group gave a general goodbye, but they all said a personal goodbye to Muhammad's father. The young ones kissed his hand, and the older ones shook hands and embraced him. One cousin took out a small flashlight and said he would walk them home.

Mattresses came off a rack, and furniture moved to make space in the living room. Borrowed pajamas appeared, and I tried to be gracious, but I muttered to Muhammad that I didn't know how I would sleep without brushing my teeth. Not to mention they were going to fall out before I was forty if I didn't take care of them.

"Use your finger."

"What good is that?"

"Just put toothpaste on your finger and rub it around your teeth. It's better than nothing."

I went to the washbasin and looked around. "Where's the toothpaste?"

Weedad answered. "We're out of toothpaste. We've been using salt." She handed me a cup of water and poured about a teaspoon of salt in the palm of my hand.

It may have been better than nothing, but only marginally. I concentrated on not tripping over my borrowed nightgown and padded across the house to the living room where mattresses were made up for us. I was grumbling about this spur-of-the-moment sleepover when another volley of automatic weapon firing echoed through the house, drowning out anything Muhammad was saying.

93

Either the sudden quiet of the house made it sound louder, or it was much closer than before. Sleeping on the floor with not-so-clean teeth wasn't that bad.

I turned off the light and slipped under the quilt, enjoying the feeling of safety. I snuggled close to Muhammad. "So, what happened today? You came in with a smile on your face that I haven't seen in a while."

"I'm pretty sure I have a job."

"That's great!" I barely controlled the volume of my squeal. "Tell me about it. And what do you mean by pretty sure?"

"Don't get too excited. It's not great. In fact, it's barely good, but it will keep us fed." He paused and my excitement drained and turned to worry.

"The pay isn't good?"

"Not much about it is good, but it's a job. You see how things are. People with good solid jobs like trucking or running their own store or even teachers..."

"Teachers, too?"

"Yeah. Schools can't open with people shooting in the streets. Teachers don't get paid if they're not teaching."

"We haven't heard shooting where we live in Zarqa for days."

"We haven't heard it because we don't live in a Palestinian neighborhood. We have lots of Jordanians living all around us."

"Like those ladies in black across the street?"

"Those are Bedouins, but yes, like them and others. It never used to matter."

I thought about that for a few minutes. I remember he told me that his brother had been in business with a Jewish neighbor in 1948 when the state of Israel was established. Saleh must have still been in his teens at the time. He and the neighbor were good friends, and they owned a truck together. Their different religions hadn't mattered then, either. As bad as this was, it had the potential to get a lot

94

worse. I didn't want to think about the possibilities.

"So, tell me about the barely good job."

"It's at the Pakistani Embassy. They need a translator."

"They want a translator with a Ph.D. in political science? Aren't you over qualified?"

"Of course I'm over qualified. I'm just lucky they're willing to hire me in spite of that. The charge d'affaires said they need a translator who understands the situation and knows the nuances behind the words in the official press releases. He thinks I'm perfect."

"If you're perfect, why don't you have the job yet? There can't be many people with your qualifications walking around looking for a job."

"The ambassador makes the final decision, especially since I'll be getting more money than the last translator."

"Humph, I should guess so."

"It's still not so hot. Anyway, the ambassador had already left for the day when I finished the interview. So, I have to go back tomorrow and talk to him."

"You'll get the job, and they'll be so happy with you that they won't believe their good luck." I gave him a kiss and pulled the covers up over my shoulders.

* * *

The next morning, we had a special treat at breakfast— hummus. The local hummus seller had reopened his shop, to everyone's delight. Zahara also served up the familiar labneh and slices of the cheese we'd brought.

"Weedad! Bring the pickles," shouted Khalil, Zahara's husband. Pickles? For breakfast?

"Bless you, Weedad." Muhammad took the dish from her and set it where Khalil could reach it.

"What's that?" Not only pickles for breakfast, but shocking neon hot pink pickles! Food had no business being that color. And those sure weren't cucumber slices.

"Ahhh, *lifit*. They're pickled turnips. Delicious with

hummus. Here, try one." He took a wedge of hot pink and plopped it down in front of me. I watched to see how other people ate it. Scoop of hummus on bread. Follow with a small bite of hot pink pickled turnip. I tried it. Definitely pickle, but the salt was stronger than the vinegar taste.

"Why is it only served with hummus? It tastes good."

"It's not only with hummus. People put them on falafel sandwiches, but I guess it's just what you get used to eating."

"Just don't let it drip on your shirt. If you have an interview with the ambassador today, you don't want hot pink stains on your shirt. It's bad enough you're wearing it for a second day."

"It's okay. There's a war going on. People understand." He took another bite of pickle. "Besides, you always say I look good in anything."

"I don't remember saying that." I glanced at him sideways. "But I must admit it's true. Knock 'em dead."

* * *

The hours crawled by. I helped the women pick small stones and twigs out of the lentils. I guessed we were having lentil soup for supper. Still nothing green or fresh available in the local stores. I thought longingly of the ripe tomatoes at Um Yusef's house and wondered how long it took for scurvy to appear. Not that I was seriously worried—yet.

I had a *mahbooseh* near-triumph, which cheered me a little. I didn't actually win, but I made my father-in-law work for his third point out of five. The possibility of winning became a reality and then a goal. Someday I'd beat the master, even if I relied on luck more than skill. It was possible.

Just when I began to think something had gone wrong with celestial mechanics because no day could possibly be this long, the sun began to set. Then I started worrying about Muhammad. How could he take all day for a job interview? When he finally appeared, his broad smile told the story.

96

I was eager to leave, but I understood that he had to tell his father what had happened. Before he finished talking, his sister set a tray in front of him with a bowl of the lentil soup we'd had for lunch. He hadn't eaten since breakfast. I felt guilty that I hadn't thought to ask him if he was hungry. Zahara hadn't asked; she just gave him the food. I was learning more than *mahbooseh*.

Jamal, the driver of our car, walked in with a smile that rivaled Muhammad's. "I got the car back today. It still needs work, but it's here."

"Can he take us to Zarqa?" I asked.

Everyone seemed to answer at once. I couldn't sort out all the answers, but I heard the nearest ones. "No. You can't go out after dark. It's dangerous." That was Zahara, the worried sister. Far too cautious, in my opinion.

Jamal waved away her objections. "Sure, I'll take you. Come on before things get too hot."

"Have they started?" asked Muhammad.

"Only a little." Jamal was being cool.

"Please. I don't want to spend another night without brushing my teeth. They're growing moss."

Zahara's protests went unheard or unheeded. I was already putting shoes on the boys, and we were ready in less than a minute. I didn't want any second thoughts on this one. I went around kissing people and shaking hands, making the quickest exit I'd seen that side of the Atlantic.

I sat in the back seat with a boy on either side of me and Muhammad sat in front with Jamal. I breathed a sigh of relief as Jamal put the car in gear and we moved away from the house and began the descent toward the main road. At last! I swore never to leave home without my toothbrush again.

TURNIPS: THE UGLY DUCKLING OF VEGETABLES?

I grew up in a household that never served turnips. Consequently, I always walked past them in the grocery stores. I had the idea I didn't like turnips, even though I had no recollection of ever tasting one. I've never actually met anyone whose favorite vegetable was the turnip. How did turnips get such a bad reputation? I suppose it's like Muhammad said so many years ago, "It's all about what you get used to eating."

While I had occasionally eaten turnip greens, the turnip itself never graced my table—until I tasted them pickled.

I've been buying turnips occasionally ever since. I learned that they are very low in calories (hooray!), very high in vitamin C, and high in fiber. I chop the small tender ones into salads. I cook the larger ones and mash them with butter and salt. And I make pickled turnips.

THE LASTING POWER OF PICKLES

Pickles have been around for more than four thousand years. Cleopatra credited pickles for her health and beauty. The Roman emperors and their soldiers ate pickles. Pickles crossed to the Americas with Christopher Columbus. In the time before refrigeration, pickling was a way of preserving fruits and vegetables for long periods of time. Pickles added both flavor and nutrients to sustain people through a long winter or a long sea voyage where replenishing supplies is not an option.

A surprising variety of foods can be preserved by pickling. From apricots and asparagus to yams and zucchini, almost any fruit or vegetable you can name can be pickled. Sometimes the pickling is to preserve the food, but it is often done just to add variety and zest to a familiar food. Pickles don't stop with veggies. Boiled eggs, the famous pickled pigs' feet, and many varieties of fish and even meat can be pickled.

MAKING LIFIT

2 pounds turnips

2 small or 1 medium beet (canned beets may be used, but fresh are better)

3 cup water

1/4 cup salt

1/2 cup vinegar (I use white vinegar because I don't want to change the color, but other vinegars will work)

2 to 4 cloves garlic (optional)

1 jalapeño or other hot pepper (optional)

Photo by Vanessa Bucceri on Unsplash   Photo by Natalia Fogarty on Unsplash

Wash and peel the vegetables.

Dissolve the salt in 1 cup boiling water. When it is thoroughly dissolved, add the other 2 cups of water.

Cut the turnips. I cut them into quarters if small, eighths if medium sized. Cut small beets in half, medium beet into quarters or eighths. Keep peeled garlic cloves whole. Some people cut both turnips and beets into strips the size of thick French fries. Again, a matter of personal preference.

Use glass jars. Put the garlic and beets in the bottom, distributing evenly between the number of jars you need for the pickles. Put the turnips on top of the beets and garlic.

Once the water has cooled to room temperature, add the vinegar and stir to make sure the two liquids are uniformly mixed. Fill the jars to within 1/2 inch of the top. Put the lids on the jars, but don't tighten the lid completely. Put in a cool dark place for at least 3 days.

Voila! You will have brilliant hot pink pickles to delight your eyes and your palette at any time of day.

For great visuals, videos, and variations:
(1) http://bit.ly/PalPickle1
(2) http://bit.ly/PalPickle2
(3) http://bit.ly/PalPickle3

Hummus

Jamal put the car in gear. My sense of relief was so strong I felt my entire body relax. I took a deep breath while he turned the car around. By the time we started down the road I felt like a new woman. I strained to hear the conversation in the front seat. Jamal talked to Muhammad about the repairs and what still needed to be done.

As we came to the first bend in the switchback road that would take us down the mountain to the main road, I heard someone shouting. The shouting seemed to follow us, and the headlights caught a dark figure with a gun ducking behind a building.

"Cut the lights," said Muhammad. Then I heard the gunfire. "CUT THE LIGHTS!"

Jamal said something I didn't understand as he slowed the car, and the road went dark in front of us. From his tone of voice, it was probably just as well I didn't understand the words. The AK47s were very close.

Ibrahim and Faisal were sitting on either side of me in the back seat. I put my arms around them and pulled their heads toward my lap. "It's far past your bedtime. Put your heads down and take a nap until we get to your uncle's house." Miraculously, they didn't argue.

Muhammad twisted in his seat to talk to me. "See those lights over there?" I could barely hear his words, but I held my hands over the boys' ears anyway.

I looked where he pointed. "Yes."

"That's where the army is. They're firing at the fighters here, and we were lighting up their targets for them."

"Should we turn around and go back?" The car was

creeping forward on the steep twisting road in the pitch blackness, and I was overwhelmed with guilt. How could I put my entire family in danger for the sake of a toothbrush? I was selfish, thoughtless, and a really bad mother to do this. "It's okay. We can go without toothbrushes another night."

"No, once we get off the mountain, we'll be all right."

"Really?"

"Yes. Besides, it would be best not to drive past those guys we just blinded with our headlights. They might decide we're the enemy." His smile said he was joking, but all jokes have an element of truth.

We continued our creep down the switchback. I don't know how Jamal kept on the road because I couldn't see a thing.

By the time we reached the bottom, the boys were both asleep. The lights went back on as we joined the main road. I had a million questions, but I kept quiet. I had caused enough problems for one night. I heard bits and snatches of the men's conversation.

"The car needs new upholstery because the seats have bullet holes right through them. New upholstery would cover the holes. Nothing's wrong with the seats, but they look bad." Muhammad nodded.

The window glass wasn't as good as the original because the demand was so great for windows that they were just making a lot of them out of plain glass instead of the shatterproof glass. Jamal claimed that he made sure the front windshield was shatterproof because that had the greatest chance of being broken in day to day driving. I thought that it also had the greatest chance of injuring the driver if broken, but I wasn't going to mention it.

Jamal continued talking almost the entire half-hour trip to Zarqa. My attention wandered as the effort to hear and the concentration still needed to understand the language became too much.

Muhammad had been right. Once we reached the main

road, we had no more trouble.

When we reached Zarqa, we rang the bell and waited. The streets were dark, but they were quiet. No gun shots. Finally, someone came and opened the gate to the tiny walled courtyard that served as a front yard. In the few seconds it took to lock the gate behind us and walk the ten or twelve steps to the door, the tea kettle was already on the stove, and the family was gathering in the living room to hear the news. It was clear they had been asleep, but Jamal was a fresh face and a welcome diversion.

I put the boys to bed hearing snatches of the conversation as I moved about from bedroom to bathroom. The tales were told and retold. My language skills weren't good enough to know if they grew with the retelling or not. Either way, the audience appreciated the news.

Once the boys were settled, I found my beloved toothbrush and scrubbed my teeth until my gums were sore. The others were still talking when my head found my pillow. I don't know what time it was when Muhammad crawled in beside me.

"Can you tell me about the new job now, or are you too tired?"

"I'm tired, but there's not much to tell."

"Why did you stay so long? I thought you were just going to talk to the ambassador so he could approve your salary. Did they put you to work already?"

"He came in late. Maybe he had something else to do, or maybe it's just a power thing to make me wait. Some people are intimidated by a Ph.D. The charge d'affaires expected him to be in by nine, but he didn't show up until afternoon and no explanations were given. He asked me a bunch of questions I'd already answered, and then I read a news article to him in off-the-cuff English. He asked questions about what it meant politically, then he said I could start work on Monday."

"That's great. I'm proud of you. I mean you got a job in

an embassy. That has to mean something."

"No, I'm just a translator. It's still not great, it's barely good."

"Even a barely good job is better than nothing."

"Yeah. The job is like the Lulus."

"No. You got the saying wrong. Either the job is a lulu, or it's a lulu of a job. You can't say the job is like a lulu. You won't last long as a translator like that." I gave him a playful poke in the ribs. "Besides, even that's not using it right. If it were a lulu of a job, it would mean it was a great job."

"I'm talking about the cigarettes. Haven't you seen the Lulu cigarettes?"

"I think so. Aren't they the ones that come in beige packages?"

"Yeah. I ran out of cigarettes today, but the stores only had Lulus in stock. Everywhere I went, that's all they had. I asked the storekeeper if they were any good. He said they were better than nothing. That's what the job is—better than nothing."

I smiled in the dark and snuggled a little closer. "You're not like Lulus."

* * *

The next big step toward "normal" was the return of running water. The first day we had water, Um Yusef spent the day doing laundry. The older girls took turns helping. They had an old wringer washing machine, but the clothes were examined and scrubbed by hand before they were put in the washer. Sheets and towels managed with just the washer. Water was heated in tubs over a kerosene burner. I tried to help but was soon told to leave them to do it. I had a sneaking suspicion that Um Yusef rewashed all the clothes I washed the minute I was out of sight.

I got my first view of real house cleaning while the laundry was being done. Anyone not doing laundry worked on the house cleaning. Room by room, whatever could be moved was pushed into another room. The walls were literally hosed down, windows, floors, every surface was hosed down and the excess water was removed with a squeegee. The windows and tile floors gleamed, and there wasn't a speck of dust visible. I shuddered to think what would happen to the houses in the States if they were cleaned like this. The walls would dissolve into puddles of soggy drywall goo, and the ceilings would collapse. Stone houses survive.

Try as I may, I was not efficient with the squeegee. At one point it actually fell apart in my hands, leaving me holding a bare broomstick. That was when they asked me to take the four youngest children out to the courtyard and keep them from coming in the house until it was clean. The children didn't need me. If Um Yusef told them to stay outside, they would stay outside. It was humiliating. Obviously, I was more hindrance than help.

As soon as the water began running again, some businesses reopened. We all cheered when the neighborhood hummus maker opened. Breakfast became a meal that made me want to get up early. Hummus and falafel are good any time of day, but they really bring the sunshine at breakfast. The local dry cleaner reopened, and Muhammad began looking more presentable when he strode off each morning to join the river of people walking toward the station to board busses and service cabs to Amman.

Things looked and felt more normal each day. It was October, and schools prepared to open. We had planned to keep Ibrahim in kindergarten for a year to let him learn the language, but when we went to enroll him in school, the principal talked to him a few minutes and said he spoke as well as anyone else his age. She enrolled him in first grade.

Muhammad learned that the university was planning to open soon, and that many of the foreign professors with contracts backed out of their agreements, citing dangerous conditions. That left many departments in need of people to cover those classes, which were mainly in the College of Sciences. He made an appointment for me, and I met with the head of the Department of Mathematics. I was overjoyed to be assigned two classes to teach. It was strictly temporary. If the professors came, I would be out of a job. I didn't mind. As Muhammad said, it was like the Lulus. Any job was better than no job. At last I could be a contributing member of the household.

I asked Muhammad if the second income meant we could get a place of our own. He shook his head. "As long as my brother is missing, I have to stay. I have to do what I can." That brought us to the only bad news we had received. Saleh, Muhammad's brother was, as they say, "under a cloud." After making a gazillion trips to the army camp to inquire about her husband, Um Yusef finally learned that her husband was not just under investigation, he was in the military prison. No formal charges had been made against him, which was good, but whatever powers controlled his fate had decided that he was not clear enough to be released back to active duty.

It's almost cliche to say that civil wars split communities and pit family members against one another. It is quite another thing to see it happening. True understanding of the emotional cost was, and is, beyond my comprehension. The American Civil War split families along ideological lines and it happened before living memory, making the concept of brother against brother an intellectual concept. Black September was very different.

The large percentage of the soldiers in the Jordanian Army who were Palestinian had joined to fight a common enemy, not to fight their cousins, or even worse, their own sons. Many wore a uniform and carried a gun belonging to one side, but with hearts and minds on the other. I'm sure I was not alone in giving daily thanks that Saleh had been in charge of maintaining the tanks, not driving or riding in

106

them. He faced enough horrors being behind the lines and doing what he had to do. Others were not so lucky.

If Abu Yusef's imprisonment anchored Muhammad in Zarqa as the temporary head of the household, so be it. Considering what Um Yusef and their children must be going through, I could manage to live out of suitcases for a while longer. Besides, I hadn't cooked a meal in months, which I considered a good thing.

I wasn't even sure I could manage grocery shopping. Meat came from a butcher, chicken from a chicken man, fruits and vegetables from a greengrocer, and rice, dried beans, spices and similar things from yet another store. It dawned on me that was what the historical novels meant when they mentioned dry goods stores.

Maybe I should tag along on some of the food shopping trips. My shopping adventures had been limited, and I had not been paying attention. My excuse of not understanding enough of the language to benefit from the outings was evaporating.

Part of me wondered if we could live on hummus and falafel if we got a place of our own.

HUMMUS

*Not only heart-healthy, hummus delivers a
myriad of benefits for the mind, body, and soul.*
(http://bit.ly/PalHummus6)

I became a fan of hummus long before I learned that there were health benefits involved. Very early in our marriage, we went to visit another cross-culture couple. The Egyptian husband, like my husband, was a Ph.D. candidate at the

University of Florida. As we started to leave, they asked us to stay for a quick supper of *nawashef*. My husband's eyes lit up. It was only after he accepted the invitation that he looked at me for confirmation. Then, as now, I jumped like a trout for a fly if someone offered a chance to eat something I did not have to prepare.

"Oh, we couldn't impose like this at the last minute." My feeble protest caused a round of laughter.

"No trouble. It's just hummus and fool." Had I heard right? Fool? Everyone was still smiling, so I guessed we weren't cooking the neighborhood jester.

"Can I help?" I trailed behind the tall graceful blond who was willing to whip up a meal in minutes as she strode into the kitchen. I felt like the country mouse, ready to bow down in abject adoration.

"There's not that much to do, but you can keep me company." Great. I had been appointed lady-in-waiting. I stood and watched her gather things with smooth efficient motions. "What's hummus and fool?" That stopped her in her tracks. She stared at me, and I knew the country mouse had hay in her hair.

"You're married to an Arab, and you never heard of hummus and foul?" She pronounced it "fool," but the can she held up had "foul mudammas" on the label. The picture showed dark reddish-brown beans. In small print it said "Fava Beans."

"We haven't been married very long." My poor excuse stammered out of my mouth. I listened to my tongue rattle on and was powerless to control it. My brain had gone off on its own journey, wondering if it would be worse to eat a fool or something foul. I decided that eating fools would be one way to rid the world of them. Then I realized how foolish I was at the moment and snapped back to pay close attention to my first lesson in Arabic food preparation. I was baffled by the ingredients. At the end of the lesson, I had no more idea how to make hummus than I had at the beginning. I did, however, get a memorable lesson in how to eat "the Arab way."

Copying those around me, I broke off a piece of bread, dipped it into the hummus, and bit off the end coated with hummus. It was delicious. I secretly decided that I was going to have less trouble adapting to his food than he had adapting to ours. I dived in for a second bite.

"Put the whole piece in your mouth."

"Mmmff?" The piece was halfway into my mouth.

"Break off a piece small enough to fit in your mouth and pop the whole thing in at once."

My next try, with a tiny bit of bread, ended with hummus on my fingers. What now? I was sure licking my fingers would be more unacceptable than reusing a piece of bread.

The blond goddess laughed. "Never mind. I'll get you your own plate so you can practice." She jumped up and got a plate, put some hummus on one side and foul on the other. To my great embarrassment, everyone watched me eat the next few bites and made suggestions for improvement. Hummus could be dipped, but most of the foul beans were nearly whole and the food had to be scooped. It may have been embarrassing, but I was grateful years later when we went to Jordan and I met my new family. At least I had some idea of the etiquette involved in *taghmeece*, or eating with bread.

* * *

Americans think of hummus as a dip. Palestinians think of it as a meal. Hummus is probably the most familiar of the basic elements of a Palestinian breakfast. In Palestine it may be found on the table whenever people are gathered to eat. It is suitable at any time of day or night.

In Palestine, the main meal is served in the early afternoon. If extra people are in the house when it is time to eat, the meal can be expanded with the addition of a plate of hummus. The meal at the end of the day is often a light snack, similar to lunch in this country. Usually informal, it can also include hummus as an important element. When served as an evening meal, hummus is often topped with browned, crumbled ground meat and pine nuts.

Leila Ibrahim, in an article for the Institute for Middle East Understanding, called it a Palestinian staple, and "synonymous with Palestinian culture and cuisine" (1). She goes on to quote second and third generation Palestinians about the place of hummus in their lives. Many associate it with stories of a simpler life before the diaspora—a time when families grew, dried, and stored their own chickpeas. The dried chickpeas were boiled in a large pot. Today very few people use anything other than canned chickpeas. One Palestinian-American called hummus a piece of Arab history, saying that in the past, "it was easily available to the poor people, and it's a plentiful food that can feed many people." Another called it "a big part of her culture and always present in at least one meal."[1]

---

[1] https://bit.ly/PalHummus1

THE GREATNESS OF HUMMUS

In all of the Arab countries where I have travelled, hummus is a mainstay of breakfast and other meals. It is readily available from one of the tiny stores, often no bigger than a walk-in closet, that spring up in almost every neighborhood. Usually run by the owner and perhaps one other person, they open early in the morning and stay open late. Unlike our take-out establishments, the hummus/foul/falafel stores sell only the food. The customer brings the containers. In the early morning, children, often in pajamas, line up with dishes and coins. If a man appears with a dish, he is generally served immediately. I don't remember ever seeing a woman in the queue, but I was seldom out before breakfast. By the time we moved to Amman, Ibrahim was already six—old enough to be sent for a dish of hummus.

There are small restaurants (and I use the word loosely) that cook kebab over an open flame on the sidewalk. The smell of the spiced meat draws customers, and it keeps the smoke outside. These micro-restaurants serve meat on skewers with pita bread and, you guessed it, hummus. Often the customers are expected to use the bread to eat the meat and hummus. No knife and fork required. Sometimes the restauranteur uses an open loaf and grabs the meat right off the fire with the bread, slides the skewer out, and puts hummus on top. Instant meal ready to eat.

John Montagu, Earl of Sandwich (1718-1792) may have given the sandwich its name,[2] but the Arabs were eating food encased by bread for centuries before the earl was born.

A simple Google search for "hummus health benefits" brings up over half a million results in less than a second. Astounding! WebMD says that "all the main ingredients are super foods in their own right."[3] Doctor Axe gives eight reasons to eat it every day,[4] and a little time spent with a search engine yields so many surprising health benefits that I was almost ready to believe it was good for everything from thinning hair to ingrown toenails.

Chickpeas, the basic ingredient, is a very good source of iron. Since chickpeas are high in protein, hummus helps keep you full longer, delaying the snack attacks. It's also full of antioxidants that work to lower cholesterol and reduce risk from some cancers. High in fiber and other nutrients, it is undoubtedly a good addition to a healthy diet. I'm not the only avid fan of hummus, and like any group of fans, some tip just a little toward the extremes. "The superfood is not only heart-healthy, it delivers a myriad of benefits for the mind, body, and soul."[5] As much as I love hummus, I don't eat it for the benefit of my soul.

The word hummus means chickpeas in Arabic. One of

111

my pet peeves is hearing people talk about "black bean hummus." That's saying black bean chickpeas; it doesn't make sense. Instead, call it black bean dip with tahini, or just black bean dip. Of course, the same goes for white bean or cannellini bean dip with tahini and garlic. Both variations are delicious and make a great change of taste. My objection is not to the food, but the name.

Americans are known for their inventive spirit, and once they adopt a food, they make it their own. Hummus is a prime example of American adaptation, or Americanization. I have found recipes for hummus with a range of additional ingredients that ran the gamut from hot pepper to avocado to sweet potato and even chocolate and peanut butter. In all fairness, the recipe that included chocolate and peanut butter was not called hummus, even though it did include a can of chickpeas.

---

[2] https://bit.ly/PalHummus2
[3] https://wb.md/2YONokC
[4] http://bit.ly/PalHummus4
[5] http://bit.ly/PalHummus5

MY HUMMUS PREPARATION

I can't very well call it a recipe because, in truth, I never measure ingredients. Admittedly, this often gives uneven results. My cooking is always edible (except for the time the shaker top fell off the garlic powder into the pot—along with all the garlic powder), often delicious, and sometimes really outstanding.

Traditional hummus is simple to prepare. I use a can of chickpeas, drained of the liquid. I usually reserve a little liquid in case it is too thick, and a few chickpeas to place in the center as garnish. Add about a quarter cup of tahini, enough lemon juice to get the right taste and color. The color is a clue of whether or not you have enough tahini. It should not be the color of mashed chickpeas, but closer to the color of pale tahini. When you add lemon juice to tahini, the mixture turns a very pale off-white. Hummus should be closer to that color—very pale beige. If I have whole garlic, I add a clove of garlic. Otherwise, I use garlic powder. Zap it all in a blender or food processor until smooth. Vague, but that's how I do it. I stop and taste, adding ingredients until I like what I taste. If you can't taste lemon, you don't have enough. If you want something more definite, the internet abounds in recipes.

The garnish makes the hummus. I used chopped parsley in a cross shape that divides the hummus into four sections. If I don't have any fresh parsley, I use parsley flakes. As always, fresh is better. I make another cross of sumac (paprika may be substituted) that bisects each of the sections formed by the parsley. A few whole chickpeas in the center, and olive oil is the final touch.

A variation that makes a great winter alternative is *fattet hummus*. This dish has been described as a savory Middle Eastern bread pudding.

The three main ingredients are: yogurt, hummus, and toasted pita bread cut or broken into bite-sized pieces.

I begin by covering my baking dish with a layer of the pita pieces at least half an inch thick. Whether or not you actually toast the bread is a matter of taste. Do you like a crunch with your food? Toasting is a good idea. Do you prefer something chewy and rich with flavor? Try not toasting. Either way is delicious.

The next step is to add the hummus and the yogurt. Many people cover the bread layer with hummus and top it with a layer of garlicy yogurt. I prefer to mix the two for a single layer over the bread.

Prepare regular hummus and add enough yogurt to make a mixture that can be poured like thick cake batter. I heat the bread and hummus in the microwave while I prepare the garnish.

Brown pine nuts in olive oil. Sometimes I use a mixture of pine nuts and slivered almonds. When the hummus is hot, top with the toasted nuts, olive oil and all.

114

Thyme and Olive Oil

Life began to settle into a new normal. Things that I couldn't have imagined a few months earlier became part of my daily routine. Each day I took the student bus from Zarqa to the University of Jordan, and each day we were stopped at the same checkpoint, and each day soldiers boarded the bus. They made all the boys get off the bus. One soldier walked up and down the aisle looking at the remaining students—and me. He would glance at the identity cards or passports and move to the next person. I'm not sure why they didn't make everyone get off, but I was just as happy to stay inside as the weather turned colder.

The boys were lined up and their identity cards were checked. The soldiers flipped through books and notebooks. The underside of the bus was checked with a long-handled mirror that looked like a dentist's tool for giants.

The last day of October was the first day of the month of Ramadan. This was my first experience with Ramadan since my husband did not observe the fast, and we had been living in the States without a lot of Muslim friends. I knew it was a religious holiday and involved fasting. In my ignorance, I equated it with Lent, a month when many Christians give up something they like, and often limit their consumption of meat. Like Lent, Ramadan ends with a celebratory holiday, the Eid, where children get new clothes. I soon learned that fasting during Ramadan has very little resemblance to fasting during Lent.

The fast for Ramadan is total and complete. Nothing enters the body from dawn to dark. Those fasting do not eat

116

even a crumb of food, nor do they drink a drop of liquid. Women cannot wear eye makeup lest it get in their eye and break the fast. Lipstick is similarly forbidden. Nothing is allowed, not even medicine. Anyone who must take medication during daylight hours is excused from the fast, although the devout usually fast an equal number of days when they are able.

Everyone seemed excited. Um Yusef even seemed cheerful when she came home from shopping and told us the government was making sure all the butcher shops had meat for Ramadan. Meals had to be extra special because there was really only one meal a day. Meat every day! We hadn't seen meat in ages.

I embarrassed myself by offering my father-in-law a cigarette one afternoon while playing *mahbooseh*. He shook his head, put his hand over his heart, and said, "I'm fasting." That seemed to be a strange answer since I wasn't offering him a cup of coffee and a sandwich. The second time I offered a cigarette, he was visibly annoyed.

"I'm not offering you anything to eat. You don't swallow the cigarette."

"No, but the smoke gets in your lungs."

"Oh." I put the cigarettes away. No wonder he was annoyed. As a heavy smoker, he must find this day-long abstinence very difficult—especially if someone sitting across from him is puffing away and offering him cigarettes.

When Muhammad came home that afternoon, I followed him into the bedroom and whispered that his father was a little touchy so tread lightly. I didn't mention that I had exacerbated the situation by offering him a cigarette—twice.

"Yeah, well I'm just grateful we get off early during Ramadan. You're lucky your classes are in the morning. It's literally hell on wheels in downtown Amman. The closer to the time to break the fast, the more road rage those cab drivers show. They're yelling at each other, at the

117

pedestrians, and at their passengers. Amman cabs normally run as much on tobacco as on gasoline."

"So why does everyone still smoke? Everyone knows the first month is the hardest. Once they've quit for a month, why not just stay away so next year will be easier?"

"Are you serious? Why don't you quit during Ramadan in solidarity? Then you can just stay away since it's so easy." He pulled out a pack of cigarettes. Feeling around for his lighter, he frowned at me. "And I hope you had enough respect not to smoke in front of my father."

I felt my cheeks grow hot with my blush. I couldn't meet his eyes. "No one told me fasting was more than food." It was bad enough feeling guilty over doing just that, but now I sounded like I was blaming him for my bad behavior. "I mean, I guess you can't remember everything." It sounded pathetic, but I couldn't keep my mouth shut. "Once he explained why he wasn't accepting my offer—"

"You didn't. Really? You offered him a cigarette?"

I nodded, thinking I probably belonged in one of the lower circles of hell. "Twice."

He took another deep drag before grinding the cigarette into the ashtray by the bed. "The up side is that the sun sets early this time of year. And I amend the statement about Amman being hell on wheels. It's only…what's that place between Heaven and Hell?"

"Purgatory?"

"Yeah. It's like that. When Ramadan falls in mid-summer? That's hell."

"I thought Ramadan was a month of the year. It moves?"

"It's a lunar calendar. It moves."

"I get it. It's like Easter that moves, but only by weeks. It's always in the spring, so there's always Easter bonnets and spring flowers and little girls in starched dresses."

"I don't know what happens to Easter, but the Islamic calendar advances by ten or eleven days each year."

"*Mart Ami.*" I heard my name called. My new name,

literally My Paternal Uncle's Wife. Arabs have four expressions for aunt, depending on the exact relationship. When I first heard that, I thought it strange, but after I thought about it, it was no stranger than our own problem with step siblings and half siblings. I try not to make comparisons, but sometimes that's impossible. The only measuring tool I have is my own experience, and all I've ever known is all I've ever known.

"Gotta go." I slipped out of the room, closing the door quickly behind me to keep the smell of smoke inside. Another call came from the kitchen. "Yes?" I followed the smell of food.

"Taste this." A spoon was being pushed toward my mouth. I grabbed the hand.

"What is it?" Dumb question. What I really wanted to know was how it was supposed to taste. Was this irony? They were asking me? My husband swears I would eat styrofoam and enjoy it if someone else did the cooking, and now I'm the official taster of the family because everyone else is fasting.

"It tastes good to me." That was pretty close to an outright lie. They were cooking kofta, a dish made with ground meat, onions, and parsley. I could barely keep from gagging as I accepted the spoonful of raw meat. I had no idea how much salt it had or how much it should have. It did not taste awful—I didn't object to the taste, but the texture and more importantly, the thought of raw meat. I just wanted it out of my mouth. I swallowed it as soon as I could.

"Are you sure? It doesn't need more salt? Not too salty?"

I shook my head and pronounced it perfect, thereby accepting all blame for a potential disaster. I shouldn't have worried. Um Yusef pulled off another of her daily miracles and had a feast spread out on the stubby-legged table a few minutes before the call to end the fast. The girls poured glasses of water and handed them all around. We sat on the padded sitting mats around the low table and waited. At last

119

the call from the mosque with the beautiful blur of not-quite-synchronous near-echoes from mosques in every neighborhood of the city. The radio tucked close to my father-in-law gave the official call to prayer, signaling time to break the fast.

The first day of Ramadan, I sat back to be out of the way of the hungry people, expecting everyone to start stuffing their faces. I was wrong.

"In the name of God the most merciful," said my father-in-law. He took a sip of water, and murmurs from around the table echoed the sentence before the others picked up their own water glasses. Only after everyone had tasted water did the hands reach for food.

I breathed a sigh of relief when I tasted the kofta. It was, indeed, perfect. The football-shaped meatballs were topped by a thick layer of sliced potatoes, then slices of tomato topped the dish. It all floated in a sauce made with sesame seed paste (*tahini*) and lemon juice, still bubbling with heat from the oven. Delicious.

We ate until we could eat no more. I hadn't fasted all day, but I over-ate in solidarity. Finally, the girls cleared away the food and the men and I went to the living room to smoke. The kitchen was overcrowded, and I accepted my role. I didn't do things the same way, so I made mistakes. I was slower and took up more space than I was worth in that tiny kitchen.

The clean-up process flowed into the preparation of dessert. We never had dessert, although fruit had been served often before the fighting. Tonight, we had *qatayef*. I understood why the young ones were so excited about Ramadan. They didn't have to fast, and they had desserts. I was almost embarrassed as I accepted my dish. A cross between a pancake and a crepe, the *qatayef* was folded in half over a mound of sweet fresh cheese or a mixture of chopped walnuts, sugar, and cinnamon. Then a hot white syrup was poured over it. The syrup soaked into the pancake-crepe and burst onto the tongue with each bite. Heavenly.

Before bed, someone went out to buy hummus. "Why?" I asked Muhammad. "Only the little ones and I eat breakfast."

"It's not for breakfast. It's for the *sahoor*. The next meal will be in the wee hours of the morning. You don't have to get up."

"Are you kidding? What could be more fun? You must admit we've been a little shy on fun lately."

He smiled and shook his head. "If getting up at four in the morning is your idea of fun, go for it."

* * *

I woke up to a rat-a-tat-tat that sounded as though it was right under the bedroom window. It took less than a second to reject the thought of guns. Someone was walking down the street drumming on a garbage can! Muhammad's eyes opened. Good. He was awake and I could ask questions. "What is it? What's he saying?"

"He's telling us to get up and eat."

"That's all? It sounds like he has more than that to say." As though getting up to eat wasn't enough. I loved waking up in the early morning to the sounds of the call to prayer, but this was different. It wasn't beautiful, it was just plain fun.

"He talks about fasting and other stuff, but it's like the community alarm clock...without a snooze button. He wakes you up whether or not you want to get up." Muhammad put his pillow over his head. Never mind. I jumped out of bed and moved toward the kitchen. I helped ferry little dishes of leftovers, hummus, and all the good things that I usually saw at breakfast. The nights were chilly, and we ate around a kerosene stove, and Um Yusef heated the bread on top. Hot bread was always a treat for me, but now we added dishes of jam, halva, and something I can only describe as apricot soup, eaten like dip with bread.

121

I loved Ramadan, but the missing place at the table was painfully obvious. We all missed Saleh (Abu Yusef) and worried about him.

A nagging thought surfaced at odd moments. Was it fair to partake in the good parts of Ramadan, like the *iftar*, or breaking fast meal, and the *sahoor* without sharing the bad part of fasting? Everyone was generous and welcoming, but the thought that I might be disrespecting their beliefs took the edge off the excitement of my first experience with Ramadan. I resolved my doubts by comparing it with our own small celebrations of a religious holiday from my tradition. Was it any different from exchanging Christmas presents with my husband? The gifts had no religious significance for either of us, but still gave us the warm feelings of love and the Christmas tree graced our house with a festive air in the dark of winter.

The days turned into weeks and the end of Ramadan was near. A few nights I had slept through the pre-dawn call of the garbage can drum, but I enjoyed huddling around the stove eating without forks and knives, dressed in my pajamas. People got less uptight about things as they fell into a rhythm; the weather got colder. I looked forward to the Eid at the end of the month as much as the little ones did.

I wanted to do something nice to celebrate. I decided to take the nieces out and get them something new for the Eid. I was told that everyone got new clothes for Eid. I always feel happy when I have new clothes, so I thought I'd do the cool aunt thing and buy everyone a sweater or something. I tried to enlist Feryal in my shopping trip, but she declined. I was all bright and bouncy trying to convince her it would be fun and that I really wanted to do it.

"But I thought it would make everyone feel good to get new clothes."

"We can't wear new clothes on the Eid."

"Why not?" She looked at me as though she didn't understand what I said.

"Because it would look like we are celebrating." She paused, probably hoping for me to nod, but I still didn't get it. Wasn't that the point of Eid? Well, not the whole point. "We can't celebrate while our father is in jail. It wouldn't be right."

"Oh. That makes sense. What about Marwa and Khalid? Aren't they too young? Won't they be disappointed about the Eid? Don't they expect new clothes?"

"They'll be fine. They would feel bad to be the only ones in the family to get new clothes. Mama will explain it, and they'll be fine. They'll still get coins from all the relatives. That's what matters to them. They'll probably make themselves sick on candy."

I'd certainly stuck my foot in my mouth that time. I walked away, trying to get the taste of toes out of my mouth. I really was the crazy foreign woman. I should have known better. Note to self: you don't really understand the customs and traditions; you only see the surface, not the meaning underneath. Stay out of things you don't understand. It was good advice. Too bad I never seemed to remember it when I needed it.

Baking started days before the Eid. There were special sweets that only appeared for the occasion. Pastries stuffed with walnuts and sugar, pastries stuffed with dates, pastries covered in powdered sugar, pastries drowning in sticky syrup. Unlike our cakes and pies, these pastries have a long shelf life with or without refrigeration. They were packed away in containers, ready for company.

Muhammad's father went out each morning and walked to the center of town. He did the daily grocery shopping for the family. When I asked Muhammad if that was normal, he said it used to be. A generation or so ago, women did not leave the house alone. Muhammad's stepmother never went farther than next door unaccompanied.

"Why doesn't she go to the market with him?"

Muhammad shrugged. "Probably because she's not good at it."

"Not good at shopping? Shopping is part of every woman's DNA. We're born good at shopping." When he didn't respond, I pressed my point. "Have you ever seen Um Yusef in action? She can bargain a zebra out of his stripes. My first day at work, I picked up a couple of pounds of apples on the way home. I'd been pretty proud of myself for making the man take a few cents less than he'd asked. Then I got home and found that Um Yusef had bought six pounds of apples for the same price I'd paid for two. I'm thinking of asking for lessons."

"My aunt isn't like Um Yusef. I'm pretty sure my aunt can't count her change or figure out how much it should be if she did count it. Um Yusef, on the other hand, can tell you to the penny how much six pounds costs if you tell her how much one costs. She knows to the penny how much the other vendors are asking for the same thing. My aunt's specialty is gossip." He gave a disgusted kind of snort. "She can't even tell time."

"You're kidding." He shook his head. He was revealing the insides of the family dynamic I never would have seen on my own. Everyone in the family was as polite and respectful to the aunt-stepmother as they were to the father.

It was not just family that treated Muhammad's father with respect. The few times we had been out with him, I had noticed the way others reacted to him. Shopkeepers welcomed him to their shops with small bows; rowdy boys stepped aside to let him pass; people went out of their way to greet him. Muhammad's father wore the traditional Arab garb that always made me think of the three wise men, but he topped it with a Western style jacket, a little longer than the traditional suit jacket. His jackets were custom made and fit beautifully. He strode through town with self-confidence and a vaguely military gait. People made way for him. He was tall and proud. He had served in the police force under the British mandate before Palestine was partitioned. He never got beyond the non-commissioned officer rank because he did not suffer fools gladly and never said things just because that was what his superior officer wanted to hear. Once he was busted from sergeant to private for refusing to run a personal errand for his boss. While on active duty, he had passed written tests in both Hebrew and English and received pay raises for each test passed. He was also very proud of having been the only Arab on the British police polo team. He was a remarkable man.

The days seemed to stretch out and string together in sluggish succession as Ramadan drew to a close. I told Muhammad that I thought the students were less attentive as the month passed. He said many people tried to sleep more in the day and stay up late at night to minimize the hunger, thirst, and cravings for cigarettes. It probably contributed to mixing up their internal clocks. Even the pre-dawn *sahoor* lost its excitement. Everyone was grumpy. The women baked; the children went to school; Muhammad and I went off to Amman in wildly mismatched schedules to earn our daily bread. I was looking forward to the three-day break of the Eid.

* * *

At last the morning of the first day of Eid arrived. I rose early, hoping to get dressed and ready for company before anyone arrived. I almost made it. Muhammad's father had come from Amman straight from the morning prayer. The first guests were family members that I had met before. I parroted the words Muhammad had taught me as greeting and continued getting the boys ready for the day. I brought them sandwiches I made by lightly coating the inside of a loaf of pita with olive oil and covering it with *zaatar*, a mixture of thyme, sesame seeds and other spices and glasses of tea with plenty of powdered milk to have a breakfast picnic in the bedroom.

125

As we ate, I heard more people arriving. I had a feeling we would be "on display" again. It was going to be a long day. We ventured from the bedroom and found the hallway already buzzing with conversation. The boys were beckoned over by the nearest woman who pressed some coins into their hands. I reminded them to say thank you as I smiled at the woman and took the empty glasses to the kitchen.

Feryal took the glasses from me and told me she and Sabah would take the boys to town for the rides. I didn't know what the rides were, but it sounded like more fun than staying in the house and smiling at grown-ups.

We had a living room full of men I didn't know, and an entry full of women who spoke too fast for me to follow, so I spent as much time trying to be useful in the kitchen as possible. My kids had pockets full of coins, and I worried about them getting sick from too much sugar. Nieces took them to the shops and to the rides, but it still worried me. The nieces that were shepherding my boys were just kids themselves. I tried to get Muhammad's attention, but he was sitting with his father receiving guests.

Um Yusef split her time between the kitchen and sitting in the extra wide hallway that ran through the house like a cross. It was used as sitting space and the family seldom used the living room, preferring to sit on mats in the hall space. The women were sitting there, and I didn't recognize many of them. I felt like I was standing in a store window. It was disconcerting to understand more than I could express. The women often talked about me in the third person when I was sitting right next to them.

"Does she color her hair?"

"Is her hair real?"

The hair questions were amusing...almost. I had long very fine straight hair that hung down my back. It was light brown, bordering on dark blond.

"Did she convert to Islam?"

The answer depended on who was talking. Um Yusef

126

gave the slight toss of her head that I learned meant No. My father-in-law's wife said, "Yes, she converted." Why would she say that? She must know better. Was she ashamed of me for not being Muslim? Did she think it tarnished her reputation somehow to have a Christian in the family? Not that I was much of a Christian, either. Religion didn't play a part in my life.

Maybe I could take another trip to the kitchen. I slipped away and almost bumped into Muhammad ferrying another tray of dirty coffee cups and water glasses from the living room.

"Muhammad, I'm worried about the boys. Have you seen them? They've been gone a long time."

"They'll be fine. It's the Eid. It's the best day of the year for little boys. They get to eat candy 'til they burst—"

"That's the problem. They'll get sick if they don't have some food. Have they eaten real food?"

"The girls will watch them. It's an excuse for the girls to get out of the house and have a taste of Eid themselves. You know it hasn't been easy on them, either. Their father's been gone for months. Sometimes bad things happen in prisons, and they worry."

Yep. I just did it again. I missed the big picture, the elephant in the room. I made an attempt to smile. "Sorry. I guess I'm not used to letting my boys go out with girls."

Muhammad gave me a quick grin. "Going out with older women," he joked as he sidestepped and handed the tray to one of the older girls who seemed to be rotating on dish washing duty.

The doorbell rang. More guests were arriving. I recognized the man in the doorway. It was Um Yusef's brother, the one who had brought the tomatoes. A young teen girl and slightly younger boy came next, followed by two women carrying identical handbags. Maybe I'd get the story now.

Of course, I didn't get the story. Even foot-in-mouth

127

foreigner knew better than to ask. All I did was sit and listen. The hallway was full of women, so Um Yusef led the newcomers to the back bedroom. The single beds that lined the walls would do double duty as sofas for the day. The house was truly bursting at the seams with guests. The two sat on the edge of a bed close together, and the youngsters sat on a mat at their feet. I sat on another bed and smiled. The four of them were close together, but it was their choice. The older woman said something in a low voice, and the others laughed softly. They were comfortable. Um Yusef came back with a tray of fruit and small plates. She sat with them and the three looked more like sisters than not. It was nice to see Um Yusef smile for a few minutes with the frown lines smoothed. The youngsters interrupted occasionally, calling the women Mama, or Mama followed by a name. There was no way to tell which child belonged to which woman.

I leaned back against the wall and let the quiet conversation flow over me. I didn't need to focus to understand the words. It didn't matter what they were saying. The tension I didn't know was building inside me began to ebb away.

Everyone left by late afternoon. The children returned, flushed with excitement, but not sick. The girls made sure they ate sesame rings with thyme and olive oil. The rings were similar to big bagels topped with sesame seeds, but the bread was lighter, and they were toasty brown. Street vendors sold them in markets and around schools. Everyone likes them, and Muhammad told me he ate them every day when he was in elementary school.

There's a saying that thyme makes you smarter. Who knows? Maybe it does. My husband is certainly clever. He was the first in his family to finish high school, and he came back from the States with a PhD.

Late that night I found Um Yusef sitting alone in the living room. I recognized the look. Too tired to get up and get ready for bed, or tired but too wound up to sleep. I plopped down next to her.

"Is it always this crazy? So many people?"

"No. Everyone came because Saleh is in jail. Friends, distant relatives, neighbors, everyone. Usually fewer people come, but our day is the first day of Eid. Tomorrow is the day we visit family in Amman. We always start with our married daughters, and then Zahara."

"So everyone who wants to wish you a happy Eid comes on the first day? How do they know that?"

"Maybe because Abu Yusef is the first son? I don't know. It's always been that way since we left Qalqilya."

I could tell by her slow words that she was thinking about her words to keep them within my vocabulary. She was so thoughtful. I decided to ask. Everyone seemed to forgive my transgressions.

"Tell me about your brother."

"Which one?"

"I didn't know you had more brothers."

"Yes. They all came when you first arrived, but there were so many people talking, and you only knew a few words of Arabic. Maybe you didn't know they were brothers."

"My Arabic is still pretty bad, but I meant the one that came today. The tomato brother." That made her laugh.

"You want to know about the wives."

"Only if it's all right to talk to me about it. Sometimes I ask too many questions."

"It's all right." She breathed a sigh and patted my knee. "We were all so young when he married Samira. It was a beautiful wedding. They were so happy." Um Yusef's eyes seemed to focus on something far away. "They wanted babies. Arabs love babies. But it didn't happen. Then the whispering started."

"Whispering?" I repeated the word. It was not part of my vocabulary.

"I'm whispering," she whispered into my ear.

"Yes. I understand." I almost laughed out loud. The Arabic word for whisper is perfect—it sounds like whish-whish" Onomatopoeia? The word popped into my head direct from a high school English class. You can't even say the word without it sounding like a whisper, or a stage whisper. At least this was one word they wouldn't have to tell me about over and over again. "What did the whispers say?"

"That his blood was dirty." I understood the words individually, but the concept of dirty blood confused me. She couldn't explain that but explained what dirty meant. Any mother of small children understood dirty. "His mother begged him to divorce Samira, but he loved her. He said he didn't care what other people said. After a time, his father got involved. He was the oldest son and had an obligation to have children. Besides, his father said he was losing business over this."

"But there's no such thing as dirty blood. Unless he had a sickness..."

"No. The doctors said he was fine. Samira couldn't have children. I don't remember the reason. Maybe they didn't tell me because I was very young. Anyway, when the family claimed that they were suffering from the villagers' beliefs, he talked to Samira. She said she would not be angry if he wanted a divorce. She cried for days, because she loved him as much as he loved her." Um Yusef closed her eyes. Her mouth curved up in a small smile. He finally told his mother that she could look for another wife for him, but he and Samira would both have to agree to the choice. The new wife would have to know that she would be treated well, but Samira was the love of his life."

"And the other woman agreed?" I couldn't imagine agreeing to be wife number two. Knowing that my husband loved the other woman with his whole heart? Not possible.

"Sometimes people have unhappy situations at home—

especially girls. I don't know why she accepted. All I know is that the two women are like sisters. He treats them equally well. When he buys one some material for a new dress, he buys the other one material of equal quality. If he brings one a handbag from his travels, he brings two. Sometimes alike, sometimes not, but always equal. The children love them both and call them both Mama."

"I noticed that. I kept trying to figure out which one belonged to which woman."

"They both belong to both women. One woman birthed them both, but the other woman held her hand, and both women mother them. I've never seen them quarrel or either one say anything bad about the other one. He drives a truck and is frequently gone for days or weeks. They take care of each other. Once Samira got sick and Amal was frantic. She stayed by her bedside and took care of her night and day. I've never seen a house with more love."

Tears stung my eyes and I reached for her hand. "If you've never seen a house with more love, you should look around you. Your home is amazing! I have never seen a house with so many children and so few arguments. If love took up space, we'd all be crowded out and sitting on the roof."

ZAATAR MAKES YOU SMARTER

Zaatar makes you smarter is what my husband heard every morning as he raced out of the house to get to school on time. It was enough to make him stop his headlong rush and grab a piece of pita bread spread with olive oil and liberal sprinkled with zaatar.

Zeit and zaatar is a great favorite of adults and children

131

alike. Zeit is oil, in this case olive oil. Zaatar is ground thyme with various other things mixed in to make a flavorful topping for bread. The ground thyme that is sold in supermarkets in small spice jars is usually a dull gray. If you add a few drops of olive oil, it turns a lovely olive green. The addition of toasted sesame seeds, along with the dark red sumac spice to add a sour taste can complete the mixture. I say it can complete the mixture because it seems that everyone has her own "secret" ingredient. I had a neighbor who added finely ground coffee, others add salt, or other spices from oregano or marjoram to allspice or cinnamon.

Although "zaatar makes you smarter" may not be literally true, thyme has been used in the Arab world for thousands of years for both flavoring and medicinal purposes. Ancient Egyptians even used it in the embalming process. Much later, thyme was used to protect against the Black Death.

I cannot promise it will make you smarter, but it tastes good and it is a healthy snack. Even today, thyme is thought to have antifungal, antibacterial, and insecticidal properties.

---

[1] http://bit.ly/PalZaatar1
[2] http://bit.ly/PalZaatar2
[3] http://bit.ly/PalZaatar3 has extensive bibliography
[4] http://bit.ly/PalZaatar4

ZAATAR THROUGHOUT THE DAY

Zeit and zaatar is not only a breakfast staple, it is eaten at all hours of the day or night. Every Arab house that I know has two small bowls somewhere in the kitchen. One has olive oil, and the other has zaatar. Both are placed on the table, and a small piece of bread is dipped in the oil and then dipped in the powdered zaatar. The zaatar now clings to the olive oil. It turns a much darker green as it soaks up any excess olive oil and is popped into the mouth. No double dipping. It's a quick and easy favorite snack any time of day.

School children often take sandwiches of zeit and zaatar for lunch. I think it's the cultural equivalent of the peanut butter and jelly sandwich. It's easy to coat the inside of pita bread with olive oil and sprinkle generously with zaatar, and I never met anyone who wouldn't eat it.

The line between breakfast, lunch, and dinner blurs with the idea of zaatar bread. Sometimes called zaatar pizza or zaatar *manakeesh* or *manaqeesh*. This can be made with pita bread by spreading olive oil on the bread, coating with zaatar, and heating it in the oven. A little experimenting will find the right combination. Some people like it crispy and crunchy, others prefer it chewy. It's a little like the difference between thin-crust pizza and thicker crust pizza.

Traditionalists start with bread dough and bake the dough with the oil and zaatar. Using the fresh leaves of the plant before gives yet another variety of enjoyment. The leaves can be layered onto bread dough or even kneaded into the dough for a different snack.

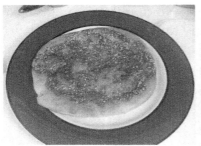

Creative Commons images from Wylio.com

Thyme leaves or zaatar can be added to traditional pizza or combined with cheese for a "white pizza." I prefer mozzarella or feta. Both the green leaves and the ground dried herb make good additions to stews, soups, potato salad, and many other dishes.

Zaatar is not confined to mealtimes. Bread dipped in olive oil and then in zaatar is a snack that is affordable, available, and always allowed. It doesn't require dishes or utensils or have a minimum serving size. It can be a satisfying lunch, or a single bite can be snagged on a casual walk through the kitchen. I have even surprised my own children dipping bits of bread into the twin dishes while I was busy putting supper on the table. Really? You can't wait a few more minutes?

Zaatar is also an omnipresent street food. Vendors park their push carts near schools and other high traffic areas, piled high with bread-like rings coated with toasted sesame seeds. If you buy a sesame ring, you also get a small packet of zaatar folded into a scrap of paper. The zaatar that is put on sesame rings has not been mixed with olive oil or other spices. It is still gray, and the only added ingredient is salt. Most people rip open the sesame and sprinkle the zaatar inside, but others break the ring in half and dab the open end into the zaatar. Delicious any way you do it.

MY AMERICANIZED ADAPTATION

I have not been able to duplicate the sesame rings, but I found two easy alternatives for *manaqeesh*. The easy and quick one is to use English muffins. Fork split the muffin, dab the olive oil all over the surface, and cover with a thin layer of zaatar. A minute or two under the broiler makes it a great snack.

The more formal alternative uses the refrigerated biscuits (like the Pillsbury Grands) found in almost any supermarket. I roll them into flat discs, coat the top with olive oil and add the zaatar. Bake as you would bake the biscuits. They're great for breakfast or served as snacks or hors d'oeuvres.

I also use refrigerator biscuits to make another snack that combines zaatar with feta cheese. The sky is the limit with this basic idea. I have seen this made for breakfast with an egg inside. Use your imagination.

Falafel

Things settled into a routine, and I thought I was adjusting well. The checkpoints on the way to and from work became part of normal. Everything was normal, well, except maybe the three Christmases that humiliated me in front of the Chairman of the Math Department. Really? Three Christmases? And every one of them fell on a day I wanted to schedule an exam.

The Christmas I'd grown up with, the December 25th Christmas, was such a low-key event as to be practically invisible. I had a couple of cards from friends that I set up on the bedside table. Muhammad was sweet and wished me a Merry Christmas, but other than that...nothing. I didn't mind. His brother was still in jail and presents were inappropriate. I should have figured that out for myself before the Eid. No one around us celebrated our holiday, and our children were too young to remember dates or even think about it without the constant commercialism that was omnipresent in the States.

I was supremely secure in my ignorance. I ground my teeth in frustration as my students told me I couldn't schedule an exam for January 7 because it was Christmas. What were they trying to pull? I was raised Catholic, and I lived my entire life in a country that considered itself Christian. I knew when Christmas was.

I arrived at work the next morning to find a note from the Chairman asking me to come to his office as soon as possible. Needless to say, I was ashamed and embarrassed to be told I was culturally insensitive, or words to that effect.

The students were telling the truth. Many of them were Christian, and most celebrated Christmas on January 7, although some celebrated it on January 6. I delayed the exam. When I tried to reschedule for January 19, the students said I couldn't because it was Christmas. A third Christmas? Surely, they were taking advantage of me. I was mortified when the Chairman told me the Armenian Patriarchate of Jerusalem celebrates Christmas on January 19. Some people learn from experience; unfortunately, I didn't seem to be one of them.

The weather got cold and wet. I slogged my way from the bus terminal to the house one afternoon daydreaming of the days when my husband was a professor, and we lived a block from the water in Jacksonville Beach, Florida. As I got closer to the house, something seemed different. It took me a minute or two to notice the open front gate, and see the people filling the tiny courtyard. What was going on?

"Come and see!" Ibrahim ran across the street and met me with a huge grin on his face. He tugged on my hand, urging me to hurry.

"What? What's happening?"

"Uncle Saleh's home!" The news burst from him like water through a hole in the dyke, then his eyes widened, and he clamped both hands over his mouth. "I wasn't supposed to tell. We were going to surprise you, but—"

"That's wonderful! It's good you told me. I need to take off my wet things before I greet him. I wouldn't want to get him all wet when I hug him." His grin returned.

"Hurry!"

I added my muddy shoes to the pile beside the door and slipped into the bedroom to spread my wet coat and scarf on the bed to dry. I knew the kitchen would be bustling with the preparation of tea and coffee, fruit and maybe some pastries. The tiny kitchen was indeed a hive of activity, but I got the breath squeezed out of my lungs by Um Yusef's bear hug. She spoke too fast for me to follow her exact words, but

137

the expression on her face said it all. The clouds might be dripping cold wet rain on Zarqa, but the sun was shining in this house.

* * *

Abu Yusef was thinner but did not show any signs of ill treatment. He did not share any of his experiences out loud. All he said was how happy he was to get back to clean clothes and Um Yusef's cooking.

Muhammad and I tried to get them to move back into their bedroom and let us sleep on the mattresses on the living room floor. They refused our offer, saying it was not practical because people came to visit and often stayed late. I felt bad kicking them out of their bedroom, but they were just happy to be together again.

We stayed.

A couple of weeks later, Muhammad came home with a huge grin on his face. "I got the job."

"Which one?"

"The journalist one with the French News Agency."

"Nothing about the university position?"

"They don't hire mid-year. Even in the U.S., they don't hire mid-year unless something extraordinary happened."

"I'd call a civil war extraordinary. I'm leaving mid-year."

"That's different. You were hired on a temporary basis. Now the people from outside can come to fill their contracted positions. They hire people from other countries in the sciences. In political science, they don't hire from outside. I think I have a good chance for next year."

"You think you'll like working with the French? You don't even speak French. Why didn't they hire someone who speaks French?"

"Probably because they couldn't find someone fluent in French, English, and Arabic. The official news releases are in English, and I'm just thankful they *did* hire me. The pay is good, and I'll get access to places with my press card."

"That's wonderful." I gave him a big squeeze. He was so excited. I couldn't tell him I didn't want him in any of those places. Fighting was sporadic, but it was still a daily occurrence. Press cards were only needed to go places with the kind of news that involved bullets and dead people.

"That's not all. I have more news."

"Don't keep me in suspense."

"I talked to a real estate guy today. He's going to show us a few places for rent. With this new job, we can afford a small place in Amman. You won't have to take the student bus and walk through the muddy streets of Zarqa. Amman has better buses and better streets and sidewalks, especially where we'll be living."

"Your work won't be dangerous, will it?"

"Walking down the street in broad daylight can be dangerous sometimes, but I promise I'll stay out of trouble."

I buried my face in his chest as I hugged him tight. "A place of our own sounds amazing." I couldn't let him see the doubt in my eyes. Would I be able to manage my own house here? I had to learn how to shop, how to cook, what money meant, and a zillion other things that were absorbed without effort as one grew up. The six months we'd been here had not given me a lot of learning opportunities. We'd been cooped up in the house, and when it was finally safe to go out, everyone was busy with school and work.

What if I couldn't do it? I blinked back tears and took a deep breath. Think of the good things. Think of having personal space again. Think of going into the kitchen without feeling like an intruder. Think of not having guests appear before breakfast. What else had I missed? Think of doing laundry by hand until we could afford a washing machine. Think of cleaning house again. Think of planning and cooking three meals a day. Think of not having anyone around to interpret my hand gestures when my vocabulary failed me. Oh, how was I going to manage?

139

* * *

The first apartment we looked at didn't work. One look at the kitchen was all it took. I shook my head. I was still trying to decide if the narrow one-pedestrian-only passage to the front door made me feel claustrophobic or safely hidden away, but the kitchen tipped the balance away from safe and hidden. I barely contained a gasp at the sight of what had been a huge hole in the wall, now nicely patched, but not yet repainted. I saw Muhammad's eyes drawn to the same area, roughly five feet in diameter on the back wall, covered in dark gray, bare cement.

"It was nothing," said the agent. "Just a stray round. No one was hurt. No one died in this house. I'll make sure it's painted before you move in. They just had to wait for the cement to dry first." The fact that he even said that no one died made me doubt the truth of the statement. A kitchen got shelled by something pretty big, and no one got hurt? Not likely. I wasn't afraid of ghosts—I was afraid of a repeat performance. This place was totally exposed to the next mountain. What if fighting escalated again?

"Let's see what else is available."

It didn't happen that day, or the next, but we finally found the perfect little apartment in a good neighborhood of Amman. The landlady lived upstairs, and a third apartment was also upstairs. We shared the ground floor with the landlord's garage, an uncommon extravagance. The narrow unpaved road had little traffic, and the house was less than a block from a main road where service cabs ran regularly.

I had to think about the logistics of setting up housekeeping on my own. All we had was what we'd brought in our suitcases and the hundred little packages of books we had shipped before we left. We needed everything—and we had very little money to spend.

Um Yusef came to the rescue again. She gave us two single mattresses and took me to the market to buy a used rug. We hauled the rug up to the flat roof and attacked it with a box of laundry detergent, a lot of water, and stiff-bristled scrub brushes.

I folded my pant legs up above my knees, and Um Yusef tucked up her dress into an immodest mini as one of the girls doused the rug and sprinkled detergent all over. We got down on our hands and knees, spaced ourselves across the rug, and scrubbed. My arms tired and my knees complained as we worked our way to the other end of the rug. I sat back on my heels to take a few breaths. Um Yusef sat back on her own heels and smiled. A scarf was tied tightly around her hair, and a trickle of sweat ran from her temple. I couldn't have done this alone. Kneeling in the middle of gray soap bubbles I had an overwhelming urge to hug this wonderful woman who rose before dawn to pray and didn't stop working until the world was quieting into night.

"Um Yusef—" I was suddenly shy. I couldn't tell her how much I cared for her, or what she meant to me. I scrambled to complete the sentence. "Can you teach me to make bread tonight? I've made bread, but it wasn't pita bread, and I always used a book." I didn't know how to say recipe.

"What?"

"A cookbook that told me what to do. How much flour should I use to make bread for our family?"

"Why?"

Now we were both confused. "When we move to Amman, you can't keep making bread for us. I have to make the bread, and my cookbooks are somewhere in all those book packages." Now the girls who were helping were staring at me, equally confused.

"I get it," Feryal said. She was struggling not to laugh. "She thinks she has to make bread because you make bread." Suddenly, we were all laughing. I never felt more a part of the family, even if I didn't understand why we were laughing, I got the idea that I didn't have to make bread. That by itself lightened my mood.

141

"You don't have to make bread. You can buy it anywhere. You have four mouths to feed. We make bread because we feed a dozen people...and the flour comes from UNRWA. We use the refugee card."

"Thank God." Did I say that out loud? It didn't matter. I grabbed my scrub brush and resumed work with a smile.

Black soapy water flowed down the rain gutters, and the rug emerged a silvery gray with a muted dark yellow pattern. Perfect. I'd thought the pattern was shades of dark gray, but I'd picked it because, unlike most of the rugs I'd seen, it was not threadbare.

* * *

The morning we planned to move our scant possessions to the new apartment, I was trying to fit everything back into the suitcases we'd brought with us, when I heard muffled cursing behind me. I turned in surprise. Muhammad and I were very conscious of our language around the children. He was shifting the book packages stacked along the wall.

"Won't the truck driver help load when he gets here?" I didn't say that he wasn't helping by moving them from one stack to another, but that's what I was thinking.

"I'm looking for those wretched papers, but I'll be damned if I can find them."

"What papers?" And then I remembered. The information on the lion cubs, or tiger cubs, or whatever the neighbor had asked us to destroy. "Oh, those papers. I'll help once I get these suitcases closed." I turned around and sat on the bag I'd over-filled. Just as I forced the zipper to round the last corner, the sound of the wake-the-dead doorbell echoed through the small house.

"Never mind. The truck's here. I just hope that if I can't find them, neither will the soldiers at the checkpoint."

How could I have forgotten the checkpoint? They stopped the bus every morning and searched it for god-knows-what. Since I never had a reason to worry, the checkpoint had become an annoyance like the mud or dust in the streets. I'd gotten so used to it. I didn't consciously think of it. "What will you do if they find the papers?"

"More importantly, what will they do if they find the papers?" He drew in a deep breath and blew it out, glancing around the room, as though the papers might have dropped out of the sky. "I'll say that I've never seen those papers before, and I have no idea what they are. Maybe my son, who doesn't know any Arabic, found them in the street and was playing with them. You know how kids love to collect stuff."

"I think you need to skip the 'doesn't know Arabic' part. Just say he can't read yet. Ibrahim already sounds like he was born here." I should have said it proudly, but my grumpy voice betrayed my annoyance. It bothered me that Ibrahim was blending in so well. As far as I could tell, he had no problems communicating, while I was still playing charades to carry on a conversation. What kind of a mother is upset by her child's success? Truly, I wasn't so much upset about his success as I was frustrated with my own lack of success.

Conversation stopped abruptly as two large men with equally large voices filled the room. Muhammad began giving directions and our books were soon stacked in the back of the truck bed, followed by the rolled-up rug, our suitcases, and a couple of boxes I didn't recognize. I was too busy keeping the boys out of the way to give the boxes much thought.

I had mixed emotions as we followed the truck away from the security of family. I was excited and looking forward to having our own place, but I was also worried about my ability to cope. I'd seen Um Yusef bargaining with the merchants. I didn't know how to do that, and I didn't have a good idea of how much things should cost.

Lost in my thoughts, I didn't realize we had reached the checkpoint until the car slowed and stopped behind the

143

truck.

"Stay in the car and don't say anything." Muhammad was talking to all of us, but he was looking at Ibrahim. "Not a word, okay?" Ibrahim nodded. They both looked at me, and I nodded as well. I thought of the papers we couldn't find, and suddenly those boy-soldiers with their man-weapons looked more menacing than they did when boarding the bus on my morning commute to the University.

The seconds ticked by one by one as I watched the drama through the windshield. Muhammad's smile looked harmless. He pulled some papers out of his pocket and handed them to the soldier.

I thought of my experience going through the checkpoint on the way to the university. The students joked that many of the soldiers held the passports upside down. Apparently, one of the soldiers heard them. The next day the soldier who boarded the bus collected all the passports and identity cards and read the name and birthplace of each student before they began the daily search. That day, it took an extra half hour to get to the University. I hoped this one could read. Don't humiliate the man with the gun.

The soldier gestured and two other soldiers got up on the truck and started looking through things. I didn't realize I was holding my breath until I gasped for air. I sat on my hands to keep from wringing them, and the minutes ticked by, one slow second after another. I began to understand why Father Time is always shown as an old man with a white beard. Cars piled up behind us.

Another small eternity passed, minute by minute. Muhammad and the soldier standing next to him were both smiling. Muhammad said something to the soldier, who laughed and flicked his hand. The two searching our possessions jumped down from the truck bed. The sun burst through the clouds, and all was right with the world as Muhammad shook the soldier's hand and returned to the car. My small family and the hidden papers crossed safely

144

through the checkpoint.

* * *

We had so few possessions that moving in was easy. We stacked the book packages against the wall in what was to be the bedroom, spread the rug in the main room, and arranged the two mattresses Um Yusef had donated to serve as couches until night when, with the addition of sheets and quilts, they would magically transform into beds.

I unpacked the boxes I hadn't recognized, grateful to find some basic kitchen supplies. Um Yusef had also packed some jars of tea, sugar, some homemade jam, and even some labneh for us in an old orange crate. The crate was soon flipped over to serve as our table.

Less than an hour after the men unloaded the truck, I had water on the stove for tea, and we told Ibrahim he was free to explore the neighborhood. He had strict instructions to stay in our little alley. We sank onto one of our bedouin-style couches and sipped our tea. Muhammad put his arm around me, and we watched Faisal scatter his toys from one end of the room to the other.

"I guess I'm not the only one who feels comfortable here. I hadn't realized how much I missed having personal space." I snuggled into Muhammad and inhaled a deep, contented breath. "I feel so safe in our own little apartment."

Muhammad didn't answer. I looked up and saw a frown on his face. I opened my mouth to ask him why he looked worried, but Ibrahim came bursting through the front door. His expression of pure joy and excitement chased all thoughts of Muhammad's worry out of the room.

"Baba, Mama, guess what I found?"

"Treasure?"

"Of course not, Mama. You know I don't have a shovel."

Muhammad mirrored Ibrahim's expression and tone of voice. "Yes, Mama. Treasure is always buried. That's why they call it buried treasure." He motioned to Ibrahim. "Come

145

over here and tell us what you found."

Ibrahim's eyes sparkled as he struggled to keep the suspense in his announcement. He let the words out one at a time. "We...have...our...very...own..." He paused and took a breath. "Falafel shop!" He looked as proud as though he had built it himself. "And that's not all. They also sell hummus."

"You are so clever to find it." I meant every word. I had no clue what to feed my family, and no idea where to get it if I did have an idea. Now I was, for the moment at least, truly content.

"And that's not all I found. There's a *furun* right next to it!"

"What's a *furun*?"

Ibrahim gave me a don't-you-know-anything look. "A place where they make bread."

Hummus, falafel, and fresh bread. I gave Ibrahim a big hug. "You are such a good finder."

* * *

A few days later, Ibrahim came in from playing before I called him. I asked if he wanted a snack since Muhammad wasn't home and supper would be a little late.

"No, thank you. I just had some cookies."

"Where did you get cookies? You know you can't go into anyone's house without asking me first."

"I wasn't inside. I was sitting on a blanket with our guards."

"What guards?"

"The ones that stand at either end of our street with their RBGs guarding us. The ones who are waiting their turn sit on blankets at the bottom of the street, and they move their Klashins off the blanket to make room for us."

I took a deep breath. I knew what a Klashin was—the short version of Kalashnikov or AK 47. I wanted to ask what an RBG was but decided to wait and ask Muhammad later.

I needed to know more about my six-year-old sitting around with automatic weapons. "They gave you cookies?"

"They always share." He started toward the bathroom but called over his shoulder. "Don't worry, Mama. They aren't strangers. I know the good guys from the bad guys."

I wasn't worried about the cookies. When he emerged from the bathroom, I tried to be casual about the guns.

"You sit next to the guns?"

"It's okay. Hamdan taught me all about what I can touch and what I can't touch and to put the bullets back exactly where I got them."

Another deep breath. "Who's Hamdan?"

"The guy who lived next door in Zarka. You burned his papers, remember? I used to go with Feryal and Sabah when they went to see his sister."

"And he taught you about Klashins?"

"Yeah. The girls would be jabbering girl stuff in the living room, and the guys would be playing cards at the table. I played under the table and made cities and roads with the bullets."

* * *

I wasn't sure what Muhammad's reaction would be when I repeated the conversation to him after the boys were asleep that night, but I never expected the delighted laughter he tried to keep quiet.

"He'll be just fine. He's already speaking English with an Arabic accent. It's not RBG, it's RPG, but Arabic doesn't have a P. They're rocket propelled grenade launchers, or RPGs."

"But what about sitting around with guns and playing with live bullets?"

"He seems to have listened to Hamdan and takes gun safety seriously. As for playing with bullets, it's perfectly harmless. Bullets don't go off by themselves."

"What if they're dropped?"

"They still won't go off by themselves. Trust me. I was trained in the Arab Legion when Glubb Pasha was in charge."

"If you're sure."

"I'm sure. Ibrahim is handling this perfectly. Think about the kids of that schoolteacher in Zarka. They'll likely be traumatized for life by the experience. Ibrahim is adapting to his new reality."

"So I should let him sit with the guards? And why do we have guards anyway?"

"Ibrahim may think they're guarding him, but they're guarding the back door to the camp. A lot of the fighters live in the camps. That's where they live and where their families live. They are guarding their fellow fighters and their families that live down in that valley."

"I see them when I go to buy bread." I took the empty tea glasses to the kitchen, still trying to digest the idea that my son was all right being near the machine guns.

"You are, too," said Muhammad when I returned.

"I am what?"

"Adapting perfectly to your new reality. You are doing a great job."

"Thank you." No need to add that I didn't feel half as confident as he seemed to think I was—not with every meal a challenge and every conversation a mine field.

FALAFEL

It is now widely accepted that civilization emerged independently in more than one location, but the Fertile Crescent, ancient Egypt and Mesopotamia, is certainly one of the earliest places where civilization arose, over five

148

thousand years ago. The birthplace of falafel, like many other foods of the Middle East, is shrouded in antiquity, but Egypt has nearly universal acceptance as its place of origin.

Falafel, like hummus, needs little or no introduction to the Western world. It has been publicized, popularized, and politicized. Falafel reigns supreme in the exact center of what is probably the most intransigent political problem in the world today. Given the close connection between food and culture, it should come as no surprise that falafel is politically divisive.

Haaretz, a well-known Israeli newspaper, published an article about falafel stating, "No matter where it originated, falafel is still Israel's national food."[1] Statements like this are countered by complaints from the Arabs that Israel is co-opting their food, traditional dress, and sometimes music. An article in *History Today* states:

> More often than not, arguments about the origins of falafel are refracted through the lens of political rivalries. Particularly for the Israelis and the Palestinians, ownership of this most distinctively Levantine dish is inexorably bound up with issues of legitimacy and national identity. By claiming falafel for themselves, they are each, in a sense, claiming the land itself – and dismissing the other as an interloper or occupier.[2]

Falafel is often classed as a street food in the Middle East.[3] In many Western restaurants it is listed with the appetizers, or with sandwiches. When used as a sandwich filler, it is topped with chopped tomatoes and lettuce, sometimes onions, hot peppers, and almost always a creamy tahini sauce. My first introduction to falafel was as a breakfast food, served with pickled vegetables and often alongside hummus. Similarly, it can be part of the light evening meal or just a tasty snack.

What exactly is inside those golden-brown balls of

goodness? The basic ingredient is either chickpeas, fava beans, or a combination of both. Egyptians tend to lean toward fava beans, but it often depends on which is more readily available locally. Almost all recipes include onion, parsley, a bit of garlic, cumin, salt, and more than a touch of pepper. It's all up to the cook and personal preference.

Falafel is very high in protein. Legumes, which include beans, were among the first cultivated plants in the Mediterranean. They were also one of the first domesticated plants in the New World, appearing before 6000 B.C. Beans have among the highest protein content of all plant foods. "The amino acids found in beans are perfectly complemented by those in cereals, and these two foods are the first ones found preserved in archeological sites. When we see Mediterranean dishes with wheat and beans, or rice and lentils, or maize and peas, they are dishes that come very close to fulfilling our protein needs."[4]

---

[1] https://bit.ly/3iyfDvu
[2] http://bit.ly/PalFalafel2
[3] Street foods in Jerusalem http://bit.ly/PalFalafel3
[4] http://bit.ly/PalFalafel4

MAKING FALAFEL

Even though each cook, and sometimes each batch of falafel is individual, the basic ingredients and steps remain the same. Falafel should start with dried beans that have soaked overnight. Each ball, patty, or fritter should be crisp on the outside and soft and crumbly on the inside. Canned chickpeas will not give the desired results.

Ingredients:
1 cup dried chickpeas (garbanzo beans)
1 bunch Italian parsley with large stems removed

1 medium onion
1 clove garlic
Salt
Pepper
Cumin
½ tsp baking soda
Other ingredients are optional: sesame seeds, cayenne pepper, thyme, cardamon, coriander, allspice, cilantro, sumac.

Oil to fry the falafel. Professionals deep fry it, but I use just enough oil to cover at least half of the falafel pieces so I can get them even brown with one turning.

Plan ahead: Soak the beans overnight.

Make the dough:
Rough cut the onion, garlic, and parsley (which some cooks mix with cilantro) and chop in a food processor until minced. Remember to stop periodically and scrape the sides to make sure the mixture is even.

If you dump everything in together, the beans will be pureed before the other ingredients are cut fine enough. The spices can go in at any stage. I usually add them with the beans, but it doesn't matter. Add the drained chickpeas and or fava beans and process until you have a granular mixture resembling coarse wet beach sand. Stop often to scrape and mix, checking the consistency. If the mix is over-processed, the falafel will be mushy.

Form the falafel:
The mixture will be rather crumbly. The dough will have to be pressed into shape rather than rolled and cut. Specialty stores sell molds; many people use melon ball scoops; you can press the dough into a rounded mound on a soup spoon, or just form a small ball an inch or slightly more in diameter between the palms of your hands. If you want

151

wider diameter, flatten the balls for better cooking.

Cook the falafel:

Heat the oil until a small sample of dough turns brown within a minute or so. If you have a thermometer, heat to 350 degrees. Lift the formed dough with a fork or slotted spoon and lower gently into the hot oil. Do not crowd the pan. Make sure they turn and brown evenly.

Photos by Daria Nepriakhina on Unsplash

If the mixture refuses to hold its shape when lowered gently into hot oil, you can add a tablespoon of flour or breadcrumbs, but this is not recommended. Either of these fillers will add gluten to an otherwise gluten free food, and they may also make the falafel less fluffy. A few more pulses in the food processor may solve the problem. Chilling the mixture also helps keep it together.

If you are adamant about not frying, you can bake the falafel on an oiled sheet. If you do this, remember it is the oil that browns the surface and gives it crispness. You have to brush the tops with oil. Again, it will work, but moves out of the realm of traditional falafel.

Photo by Anton on Unsplash

Photo by Pille-Riin Priske on Unsplash

Foul (pronounced fool)

The next morning, I woke up with a warm, safe glow. What could be better than waking up snuggled close to Muhammad on a single mattress? Across the room, the boys were sprawled on their mattress in a tangle of limbs and blankets. The morning routine went as smoothly as could be expected, considering it was the first morning in a new house, and the boys were excited about going to a new school.

We all walked to the small private school, and sat in the principal's office We explained that Arabic was the second language for the boys and we would appreciate an honest opinion of our best options. After a short conversation with Ibrahim, the principal decided to continue first grade. Faisal was only two, but the principal said she would take him. I just needed to pack some spare clothes in his backpack. I missed most of the conversation because of my limited vocabulary, but Muhammad seemed satisfied. He gave the boys a short lecture on being good for the teachers. I hoped the nursery schoolteacher was prepared for a very active two-year old whose potty training was far from perfect. We left as the boys were being led to their respective classes.

"In case you missed it, we will bring them to school in the mornings and the bus will bring them home." I nodded my head in understanding. "They'll need uniforms, so you might want to take care of that today." He raised his hand and a passing service cab stopped for him.

"Wait—"

"Can't. Sorry, I'm already late for work. I'll see you this

evening." The cab moved away, leaving me feeling totally alone. I was reasonably sure I could find my way back to the house, but then what? Uniforms? Take care of it? How?

It was a little confusing to me, but the boys had to wear uniforms over their clothes. Girls wore uniforms of blue and white striped dresses with detached white collars through elementary school, after which they switched to green and white. Boys in public schools did not wear uniforms, but boys in private schools often did. In the lower elementary grades, their uniforms used the same blue and white striped fabric made into long-sleeved smocks rather than dresses. As non-citizens, our boys were not eligible to go to public school, not that we wanted them in the overcrowded classrooms of the public school system.

I was walking home, still pondering the uniform puzzle, when I passed a chicken shop. That was handy. I decided to lift my spirits by fixing a chicken dinner that night. I stepped into the shop that reeked of chicken poop. My entrance started a chorus of complaints from the chickens jammed into crates on the way to dinner—our dinner, not theirs.

"I'd like a chicken, please." The man came out from behind the counter and went to the stack of crates.

"Which one?"

I couldn't see any difference between one white clucking chicken and the next. I raised my hand and pointed in the vague direction of the crate at eye level. "That one." He thrust his hand in and the noise intensified.

"This one?"

"Yes." I could only see his back from where I stood, but whichever one he chose was fine with me. He carried the flapping chicken into the back room, and after a short pause, I heard a rhythmic thunking sound. I'd seen the machines they used to pull the feathers off the chickens, large rotating drums covered with hard rubber protuberances shaped rather like inverted shot glasses. I had no desire to see one in action.

"Do you want the legs?" he shouted from the back.

"Yes." What good is a chicken without drumsticks?

The man returned with a small brown paper bag and told me how much. I handed him money and held out my hand for the change. He misunderstood and put the bag in my hand.

I couldn't suppress a yelp as I jerked my hand back, dropping the recently deceased chicken to the floor. I knew that all birds have rapid heartbeats and high body temperature, but that had nothing to do with food. When that bag hit my hand, it was really hot. The chickens I bought were always cold and wrapped in neat packages.

Embarrassed, I reached down and picked up the folded top of the bag with the tips of my fingers. "Sorry," I said, avoiding the shopkeeper's eyes as I scooped my change off the counter, and fled for the fresh air.

I hurried home, worried the paper bag might get soaked and spill chicken parts all over the sidewalk. Relieved that the bag was still dry, I plopped it on the kitchen counter and peeked inside. I yelped and dropped the bag...again.

There she was, looking back at me. Her head was cocked to one side, and she stared at me out of one beady black eye. Her curled talons seemed to be trying to take revenge for her early demise. My stomach churned and my breakfast threatened to come back for an encore. There was no way I could cook that dead animal. We'd had falafel and hummus for dinner last night. We could have foul tonight.

"Um Nabeel," I called to my landlady as I knocked on her open door. She popped her head out of the kitchen and motioned me in. "Would you like chicken for supper?"

"No, we're stuffing squash." She and her mother-in-law were hollowing out small green squash in preparation for dinner. I was still holding the bag between my thumb and the tip of one finger wondering what to do with it. Um Nabeel looked over at me. "What's the matter?"

I told her the story. Maybe if I hadn't supplemented my

156

meager Arabic with gestures of a dead chicken with curled claws, they wouldn't have laughed quite so hard. She took the chicken from me, trashed the head and feet, and washed it under running water with olive oil soap. When she was satisfied that the smell was gone, she rinsed it thoroughly before rubbing the surface, inside and out, with a mixture of flour and salt. She rinsed that off and put the chicken on a clean plate. She handed it to me with a smile. I said a simple thank you because I couldn't figure out how to mime "miracle worker."

"What else can I do for you?"

"You could tell me where I can buy school uniforms." The laughter was more subdued this time.

"You don't buy school uniforms. You buy the material. I'll find a dressmaker for you, if you like."

"No, I think I can manage. Where can I find the material?" A dressmaker sounded far too expensive. I'd been sewing since I was big enough to handle a needle. I'd been sewing some of my own clothes since I was in junior high.

The government approved material was the only rule. Other than that, the cut and design was up to the individual. I wasn't worried about sewing the uniforms, but I was worried about buying the material by myself. How could I get a good price? What if I got lost coming home? Um Nabeel misread the expression on my face.

"Don't worry. The shooting never starts this early."

Shooting? That hadn't even occurred to me. Another item on my worry list.

"How much should I pay? I'm worried about money."

Following Um Nabeel's instructions, I caught a bus downtown and bought what I needed. I probably paid more than I should, but I still felt a thrill of accomplishment. Then I hurried to get a bus home. It was getting close to time for the boys to get out of school. Happily, I boarded a bus that had half a dozen people standing in the aisle. If I missed this one, who knew how long it would take to fill the next bus. Buses never moved until they had a full load. Schedule? Who needs schedules?

It took a few seconds to notice that everyone was looking at me, and the bus driver was talking to me, or was he yelling at me?

"The bus is full. Wait for the next one."

"There's room." I gestured to the near-empty aisle. "I'm 'okay.'" Everyone knows the word "okay." I showed him my grip on the seat next to me.

He didn't seem to understand me. "Woman, get off the bus."

Finally, I got the idea. It was all about being a woman. I tried to say my children were coming home from school.

He said the same thing again, only louder. Louder always helps, doesn't it?

I wanted to get home, but could I really stand up to the pressure of all the riders who also wanted to get home? The driver wasn't moving. I muttered something about third world countries and started moving toward the door. A man got up and blocked my way. He gestured to his seat. I smiled at him, thinking for the second time that day how inadequate "thank you" sounded. I sat and the bus lurched forward.

* * *

Back at home, I rushed to get the fabric cut before anyone else got home and I had to worry about other things. Approximating size by using a shirt from each, I was stitching pieces together before I realized the boys were a lot later than I'd expected.

My mind flashed to last night's conversation with Muhammad about the droning radio program he'd been listening to. "What are they saying?" I'd asked him. "It sounds like someone's reading his laundry list."

"They're reading the names of children who are safe,

and then telling us where they are."

"Santa's list."

"What?"

"He knows if you've been good or bad—who's naughty or nice. Who's safe and who's not."

"Well, it's not Santa's sleigh. It's school buses that got stranded while taking children home. If the fighting gets too close or too heavy near the route, the driver may decide it's not safe. He stops in a neighborhood and parcels the kids out to people willing to take them in for the night. The kids get fed and a place to sleep, and someone gives the list of names to the radio station, so the parents know they're safe, and where they are."

"Maybe they shouldn't have opened schools yet."

"The government has been claiming that 'law and order has been restored' throughout the country, with only a couple of resistance strongholds. So...they had to open schools."

In my naïveté, I had assumed we had nothing to worry about. After all, our school was only a few blocks away, and I hadn't heard any gun fire. But my children were very late.

I took my sewing outside and sat on the front steps. I was cold, but I could see the length of the alley. My hands had trouble holding the needle. I told myself I was shivering from the cold, but my hands could have been shaking from fear. I felt so helpless. I had no idea what to do. Where were my babies? At last, I saw Ibrahim coming up the alley, pulling Faisal with him. Ibrahim's face was red with the effort of his hard work. Faisal had spotted something he wanted and was working equally hard to free his hand and pick up the object. Why didn't the bus bring them home? A first grader can't be expected to control a two-year-old who is fighting to get away from him. My heart went out to the big-brother effort Ibrahim was making. I could tell it was taking every ounce of his strength to pull his brother along, and I was so proud of him for his responsible behavior. I dropped my sewing and ran to meet them.

"Why are you so late? Did something happen to the bus?" I hoisted Faisal up on my hip, realizing a little too late that he was wet.

"We aren't late. We're just the last ones on the ride. We go all over dropping everyone off, and then the driver brings the bus home. He lives down there." Ibrahim pointed to the forty-five-degree slope of rubble and loose rocks at the end of the alley. It looked like a mountain of construction rubble with dangerous footing.

"You walked your brother up that gravelly slope to get to our street?" From the end of the alley we could see the tops of the tiny houses nestled cheek by jowl in the strip of land below us. There was no road between the two neighborhoods. The steep difficult slope separated us from them. They were the refugees living in block houses with few if any amenities, and we were the privileged ones living in quarried stone houses with electricity and running water.

FOUL MUDAMMAS

Hummus and foul (pronounced "fool") are often served together. Like shoes and socks or salt and pepper, they are always referred to in the same order. I can't recall ever hearing anyone talk about foul and hummus—it's always hummus and foul.

Since the two are paired so often, why is it that foul isn't as well known outside the Arab world? One reason could be that chickpeas are more readily available in supermarkets in the West. Fava beans, the basic ingredient of foul, are seldom seen in supermarkets. Another reason might be because, unlike hummus, there is no "standard" recipe. Sometimes the beans are served whole, sometimes they are served pureed, and often somewhere in between.

Foul mudammas (sometimes written "ful medames") is a staple food in Egypt and is often considered an Egyptian dish. According to Wikipedia, the earliest evidence of the use of the beans was found in a late Neolithic site on the outskirts of Nazareth—squarely within Palestine.[1]

In spite of the fact that hummus totally eclipses foul in the U S market, foul has some avid fans, like Max Falkowitz. Max wrote a great article, "How Ful Mudammas Made Me Forget All About Hummus"[2] describing a few variations. The last sentence of his article, "You could even, horror of horrors, serve it over hummus," surprised me. Yes, I have eaten foul served over hummus, and I found it very enjoyable, as did everyone else at the table. However, I thought of it as what-to-do-for-breakfast-the-next-day. In other words, a very tasty combination of leftovers. Apparently, it's a bona fide recipe in its own right, and it has its own multiple variations and recipes.[3] Astonishing!

---

[1] http://bit.ly/PalFoul1
[2] http://bit.ly/PalFoul2
[3] http://bit.ly/PalFoul3

MY FOUL PREPARATION

Another great thing about foul is that you don't have to apologize for not starting from scratch. Everyone uses canned fava beans, except the specialty restaurants that boil the dried beans for hours to reach the correct consistency.

Empty the entire contents of a can of foul into a pot. I use a glass pot because I don't want to use my masher on any of my non-stick pots. I usually put the beans in the microwave for a couple of minutes before mashing. Make sure you cover with a lid because the beans sometimes burst and can make a mess of the microwave. If cooking over the stove, stir frequently as the beans may stick to the bottom of the pot.

Once the beans are hot, it is easier to mash them. I do not use a blender or food processor, although some people do. The beans should only be mashed enough so that a few beans remain entirely intact. The dish should retain the look of beans (not the smooth consistency of hummus).

Add some garlic, a little salt, rather more pepper than salt, cumin, and lemon juice. The reason I use very little salt is that most beans are salted when they are canned, and salt should be dominated by the pepper and lemon tastes.

After everything is combined, the mixture should be heated again and served hot. It should be nice and thick, or it will be difficult to scoop up with bread. If the lemon juice and liquid from the can make it too thin, just boil it a bit longer with the lid off. Do remember to stir frequently.

While the beans are heating, mince some mild pickled peppers. I use pepperoncini, but banana peppers are just as good. Some people prefer a stronger pepper.

Put the hot foul into bowls, top with the minced peppers, and drizzle olive oil over the top. Eat with snippets of pita bread.

Fagoose and Other Fruit

Living in a water-poor country was a new experience for me. Having our own apartment meant we were on our own and had to live within our means. Our "means" was a cubic meter reservoir on the roof. Every kitchen sink had three faucets: hot, cold, and straight from the mains. We always used the faucet tapping the city water supply when possible.

Water ran through the mains on different days for different regions of the city. The section with the fancy houses of ministers and wealthy people had running water every day, but the rest of us had to make do with whatever the powers that be doled out to us. Apparently, the largesse of the scheduler was directly proportional to the economic status of the residents. Our water was scheduled to run three days a week, but the schedule was not always reliable.

When the water did not run on a scheduled day, groups of women would come up our street with five-gallon cans balanced on their heads. The water beggars. The women knew there was an outside faucet on our house and asked if they could fill their cans.

"The water's not running today."

"But the faucet still gives some water." Obviously, they had more experience than I did with that particular faucet, so I followed them around to the side of the house and watched. At full open, the faucet gave a very weak trickle, more of a dribble than a trickle.

"That will take forever to fill your cans."

"We'll wait."

"Okay." I went back inside, giving it no further thought. Later that afternoon, when I went to pick up the boys (lest they travel through the entire city before getting home), I found the patio covered in muddy footprints. I was not happy at having to clean the patio twice in one day.

I complained to Muhammad when he came home from work and learned more about the conditions in the refugee camp than I really wanted to know. Built to house refugees from the violence caused by the creation of the state of Israel in 1948, the camps were never meant to provide long-term living facilities. The one near us was probably built in the middle of nowhere, and the city expanded in the following decades to surround the camp. The houses were mainly cement block walls topped with sheets of corrugated steel— not something capable of supporting a water tank, even if the families could afford one. The women depended on the city water and probably had enough five-gallon cans to keep their families until the next scheduled water day.

Wondering how I would cope in their place, I decided the least I could do was allow them to catch the water from my outside faucet and clean up after them if I had no alternative. After that, whenever the women showed up for water, I put out a mop and said they could get water if they promised to leave the patio as clean as they found it on arrival. It worked…sometimes.

* * *

The sporadic fighting continued. As the Palestinian forces were driven out of the cities one by one, the threat to school bus routes subsided, and the conflict lost its immediacy and relevance in my daily life. Things returned to normal over a period of months, but since I had never experienced "normal," it was a constant learning experience.

I was consumed with trying to fit into my new life. Language was a barrier, but I was making progress. I had reached the point where I could usually make myself understood. I abandoned the idea of conquering the grammar and concentrated on gathering enough vocabulary

165

to complete my daily tasks. Arabic has several sounds that I found difficult to distinguish because the variants do not exist in English. For example, the name of our oldest son, Ibrahim Hallaj, has two letters H when written in English, but the letter H in Ibrahim is not the same letter in Arabic as the H in Hallaj. Everyone was patient and often pronounced the words over and over as I tried to reproduce the two sounds, but the end result was more frustration. Why couldn't I hear the difference?

One day a niece asked me for a pin. I brought her a safety pin. She laughed. "No. I want a pin to write with."

"Oh, you mean a pen."

"That's what I said. Pin."

I repeated the two words over and over, but she could not distinguish the sounds. Why couldn't she hear the difference?

As the months passed, I got a little too confident— especially around people who were hearing my mispronunciations for the first time.

One afternoon I returned from work and waved at Um Nabeel sitting under the ancient grape vine that shaded their driveway. She and a couple of ladies I did not recognize were sipping Arabic coffee out of tiny cups. She gestured me over and waved her cup at me. I dropped my things inside the front door and joined them.

I don't know what they had been discussing, but when I sat down the silence was deafening, as my mother used to say. Um Nabeel probably said the first thing that came to her mind and asked where my husband was. He was at the university taking a civil service examination, but I didn't have the vocabulary to say that.

"He's at the university taking a test." At least, that's what I thought I said. I knew immediately that something was wrong when the two ladies who had just been introduced gasped, and my upstairs neighbor turned beet red trying to smother her hysterical laughter.

166

After a short back and forth, I found out that what I had really said was, "He's breaking wind at the mosque." I was never invited for coffee with those particular ladies again.

* * *

This was only one of my many embarrassing foot-in-mouth events. As my language skills increased, so did my confidence. Yes, I still made mistakes, but most people appreciated the fact that I was making the effort and forgave most of my faux pas. The embarrassing exceptions and the not-so-pleasant memories are still fresh and vivid.

I also worried about merchants taking advantage of my ignorance. In a different monetary system, it is difficult to know how much the money was really worth. A direct conversion to dollars and cents makes no sense (pun intended). How do I figure that out? My early attempts were based on payroll. I tried to figure out how many dinars we made a month and compare it to how many dollars we used to make per month. That gave me a rough starting point, but it was woefully inadequate. Some things sounded really cheap, while others still sounded very expensive. The magic formula was not available, but with time I was able to get a feel for the value of money. I soon found merchants that I could trust and listened to other shoppers, paying attention to what they actually paid for things.

I stopped worrying about making a fool of myself—too many other things to worry about. I had to learn to cook with unfamiliar ingredients; I had to cope with a two-year-old who refused to speak a word of English; I had to learn to buy groceries where it seemed that every ingredient came from a different shop—butcher, green grocer, corner store; spices in huge burlap bags to be bought by the fraction of a kilogram. A what? How much is that?

I had to learn how to entertain. I was at a total loss when Muhammad came home and announced, "My friend, Ismail, and his wife are coming over today. Nothing elaborate, just dropping by for some conversation in the *maghreb*." That brought up a new concept—alternative time keeping methods. Muslims pray five times a day, and these prayer times dissect the day into distinct segments. You go to work or school by the clock, but you go visiting by prayer times. In my mind it was similar to the way people in convents referred to time as "after vespers" or "before matins." It was totally meaningless to me. They might as well have been speaking in tongues. Oh, wait—they were speaking in tongues—a foreign language trying to explain a foreign culture.

"In the *maghreb*? What time is that?"

"It varies by a few minutes every day," explained Muhammad.

"That's no help. I need to know if I get the boys ready for bed before or after they come."

"Sometime in the late afternoon." Very loose, very vague—at least to me.

Then I stressed over what to serve. A non-meal visit had a certain rhythm to it. I had seen it as a guest, but it took practice to perfect the timing. An afternoon visit could start with lemonade or a soft drink. Little dishes of mixed nuts and or toasted seeds—watermelon, pumpkin, roasted chickpeas or a combination—needed to be within reach. I thought the fruit came next, or was it the cookies? Passing the box of chocolates was just before the coffee, wasn't it?

Baked sweets generally appeared at evening gatherings. The only immutable rule was: No one can leave before the coffee is served, and when the coffee is finished, so is the visit. Once I heard my brother-in-law tell a good friend to hurry up and serve the coffee because he was ready to go home. My fear was that I would serve things too soon and rush people out of the house unintentionally. Well, that was one of my fears.

FAMILIAR FRUIT REVISITED

One of the things I loved about my new home was the ever-present and ever-changing palette of delicious fruit. Fruit was on the table with all the other things put out for breakfast. It was always present in the house, and it was always there for snacking and dessert.

How to serve the fruit was an enigma I unraveled over time in bits and pieces. Some fruits could be served together, others not. Some were suitable to serve to guests, others not. I was raised in a culture that seldom served fruit to guests. Dessert was pie, cake, or some other sugary concoction. Perhaps it wasn't so much the culture as my immediate family. Either way, I had never given any thought to serving fruit. Fruit sat in a fruit bowl and looked pretty. It was not something that came to mind when planning for the arrival of company. My attitude changed quickly, but the implementation was a slower learning process.

I often said my boys and I may have been the only people to have benefitted from Black September. Our time sequestered in a small house with a large family gave us a forgiving space to try out our wings as we coped with a new culture, a new language, and a new way of life. With the schools closed, the older girls could pass the time with chit-chat and helping my vocabulary grow. Social life was confined to daylight hours, and fancy gatherings were suspended. I enjoyed the proverbial silver lining. Not everyone was so lucky.

One of my American friends, whose Jordanian family occupied the social stratosphere of wealth and politics, shared one of her most embarrassing moments. She'd been invited to an elegant dinner party and the hostess served beautiful crisp red delicious apples for dessert. Each guest

169

was given a small plate with a big shiny apple flanked by a sharp knife. At last, something familiar. Her mouth watered from the sight. Her Arabic was not yet fluent enough to follow the conversations flowing around her, so she picked up her apple and took a big bite, enjoying the satisfying crunch. The room was suddenly silent. Conversation stopped mid-sentence, and everyone was frozen in place. All eyes were looking at her.

"I was very new in the country," she said. "I was mortified. How was I to know I should use my lap as a table and cut the apple into bite-sized pieces before popping them into my mouth? Can you imagine anything worse?"

Yes, I could. I immediately had visions of trying to cut an apple while balancing a tiny plate on my lap. I pictured the apple's smooth round sides sliding out from under my knife and rolling off the plate and across the floor. That would be worse, and I could almost feel how the knife would slip.

I decided to slot apples into the "family only" category. Children could grab an apple for a snack and chomp away like children anywhere. Adults in polite company did not do that. Even the apple, which I had eaten all my life, had serving etiquette. Sometimes it was overwhelming.

Apples and oranges go together in my mind like salt and pepper. I soon learned that oranges weren't any easier. I spent years in Florida and enjoyed eating oranges, although I never enjoyed peeling them. Peeling oranges had always been a messy and bothersome ordeal. My experience was either using fingernails or peeling the orange with a knife much as one would peel a potato.

I soon learned that peeling an orange can be an art. Oranges, like apples, were served on a plate with a sharp knife. I learned to make cuts in the peel resembling longitudinal markings on a globe. Then slice off the top. Removing the strips of peel from the fruit becomes a reasonably clean operation, after which the segments can be easily separated and arranged on the plate like the petals of a flower.

Melons became my favorite fruit to serve to guests. It was safe and easy to handle if served properly. To present a bowl or plate of melon, the fruit had to be cut into bite-sized pieces, and all seeds had to be removed (this was before the advent of seedless watermelons). To this day, this is the only way I serve melons, often mixing watermelon, cantaloupe, and an occasional honeydew.

The first time Muhammad and I stopped at a roadside stand to buy melons, I wavered between shock and dismay. The huge pyramids of fruit looked familiar from a distance, but upon closer inspection, they were just a bit off. When we left the States, all the watermelon in the supermarkets were long—at least twice as long as their diameters, and usually three or four times longer. All the watermelons in the roadside stand were spherical. On the other hand, my "normal" cantaloupe was nearly spherical, but the cantaloupe in Jordan were elongated. Bizarro. I had not noticed before since I had only seen the fruit served in bite-sized pieces. Fortunately, the fruit itself looked and tasted as I expected.

Grapes, too, had an etiquette of preparation. The large bunches had to be cut into smaller bunches with three to ten grapes per bunch. The stems on each of the tiny bunches had to be trimmed to make sure no little stems remained from which the grapes had fallen or been removed. This makes a neat and appetizing presentation.

Unfortunately, I had a personal problem eating grapes in public. The grapes almost always had seeds, and the only way I could eat them was to swallow the seeds like aspirin. I preferred eating grapes at home where I could remove the seeds from my mouth and put them on the side of my plate. The family laughed at my eccentricities, but I knew others would not be so forgiving. Both cultures probably agree with my mother that once it's in your mouth, you swallow it—no

171

matter what. The rare exception should be removed in a way that no one else knows.

WHEN DOES UNFAMILIAR BECOME EXOTIC?

Some fruits I had never seen before, such as the *fagoose*, or Armenian cucumber. It looked like a pale cousin of the small dark cucumbers favored in the area, but the fagoose were much sweeter and had fewer, softer seeds. They were never peeled and usually eaten without the need for knife or plate. The boys loved them, and I never objected to them as a snack. I occasionally chopped them into a salad, but the family considered that a waste. For some reason, fagoose was a "family only" snack and never served to guests.

Fagoose was not the only "family only" snack. Large citrus like grapefruit and pomelo were not served to guests. That didn't surprise me because I classified grapefruit as a breakfast fruit, and I was mildly surprised when it was served in the evening as well. Pomelo was another fruit I had never seen before, although it easily slotted into place beside grapefruit. I watched as my sister-in-law peeled the fruit in the same way she peeled oranges. Then she deftly opened the individual segments and removed the tough outer covering, filling a bowl with easy-to-eat pieces of delicious fruit.

Muhammad's sister had planted a loquat tree when their house was first built. By the time I saw it, it had a trunk six inches in diameter and supplied the entire family with fruit.

The loquats were delicious. I don't know how much of the taste was the knowledge that the fruit had been hanging on the tree only minutes earlier, but the taste was wonderful. The fruit itself was about the color of apricots, but about a third the size. The skin was smooth and resembled a plum in texture. The one or two shiny brown seeds cluster in the center.

It seemed to me that loquats weren't grown commercially. Even the ones we saw in the green grocer's looked as though they had come off someone's back yard tree that very morning.

Pomegranates were something I was familiar with but had never seen or eaten. In our house, this fruit was only eaten at the kitchen table. The reason for this is that pomegranate juice stains clothing and removing the fruit from the hard outer shell and tough inner membranes is difficult and messy—a chore not to be expected of guests.

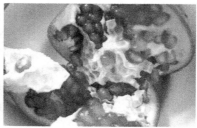

Bryan_T flickr via Wylio.com   Lindsey Turner flickr via Wylio.com

173

In season, pomegranate juice was available from street vendors One vendor, anxious to sell his wares, told us it was the "Arabian Viagra." We shared a laugh. I thought perhaps he believed it, but it's hard to tell. Today both the fruit and the juice can be found in supermarkets, and the juice is advertised as heart healthy. I haven't seen anything claiming the Viagra-like properties, but you never know.

Sara Bender via flickr.com   Miguel Urieta via unsplash.com

Prickly pears, another food that I was aware of but had never eaten, was greatly appreciated by almost everyone in the family. I tried to fix them once and vowed never to do it again. The small, almost-invisible thorns preferred my hands to their mother fruit. The women who sometimes sold fruit door to door would clean them for me if I asked, so I never bought prickly pears from the market, but waited for a vendor to pass the house. She would turn on the outside faucet and rub the fruit with her bare hands under the running water.

Every time one of these vendors told me that the water washed the little thorns away, I smiled and tightened my grip on whatever container I'd brought to carry my purchases inside. Their work-hardened hands made me almost embarrassed by my privileged soft hands. As far as I was concerned, the fruit wasn't worth fighting the thorns, although that was not based on taste, but mainly because it was another fruit that everyone ate seeds and all.

David Schiller via flickr.com   Joseviparra via Pixabay.com

Green almonds, something else entirely unknown to me when I lived in the U S, became a family favorite. The almonds are picked as the nut itself begins to form, when it is almost the consistency of a cucumber seed, and not much bigger. The future outer husk of the nut is what we eat. Green almonds have a very short season and must be harvested at exactly the right time. If the nut is allowed to mature on the tree, the fibrous outer husk becomes inedible. As the nut matures, the husk dries and cracks, leaving the almond to be harvested as a nut. However, harvested early enough, the immature almond can be eaten in its entirety, green husk and all. Simply delicious. Dipped in salt and popped into the mouth in one or two bites, green almonds are healthier and more addictive than potato chips.

Ripe fig picked from one of our fig trees

Figs beginning to ripen   Fig tree in our yard in Virginia

Before moving to Jordan, my only experience with figs had been inside fig newtons. Muhammad insisted that figs should be eaten the same day they are picked, the sooner the better. We bought mountains of figs from street vendors, usually women who had picked them from their own trees. Figs were more versatile than many other fruits as they were a family favorite but suitable for company. Figs had to be fresh and flawless to be presented to guests, although if they were less than perfect, they could still be served to close friends who dropped by unannounced—if any survived discovery by my men folk.

Guavas, peaches, apricots, mangoes, bananas, and more types of citrus than I had names for came and went in the appropriate season. The best part was the taste. In water-poor countries, crops are carefully and minimally irrigated to save water. Fruit also remains on the tree longer because it does not have to travel long distances, nor does it get stored in ways that inhibit the ripening process to allow sales after the natural season has passed.

Photo by Dennis Jarvis via flikr

Many years later, when we returned to the United States, my youngest son, then six years old, asked why the fruit tasted so much better in Palestine. His father answered, "Because Palestine is the Holy Land." No one contradicted him.

Epilogue

My husband signed a contract to teach at the University of Jordan the following year, and one spring day he took me to the American Embassy for an interview. Jordan had been declared safe enough for the families of the American diplomats to return from Greece, where they had been housed during the hostilities. The American Community School was ready to reopen, and the embassy was recruiting teachers. I was hired to teach math and science. It was a dream teaching position. The embassy was generous with its budget and my requests for materials to use for science were never questioned. The classes were small and discipline was manageable. We had found our place.

On July 17, 1971, Faisal's third birthday, the remaining Palestinian forces moved out of Jordan and set up shop in neighboring Lebanon. This marked the official end of the conflict.

* * *

Four years passed. Muhammad and I continued our teaching and added another son to our family—Mazin. Three boys meant I was accepted by even the most hard-nosed Arabs. I gave my husband sons. Even the cleaning lady at the hospital gave her approval.

"Are you married to an Arab?"

"Yes."

"Is he married to anyone else?"

"No."

"Just you?" She looked askance at my 110-pound self

barely visible under the blankets.

"Just me."

She continued to mop the floor for another minute or two. "Just you?" she asked again.

"Just me."

She shook her head. "Do you have children?"

"Three boys."

"Oh. Three boys. All boys?"

"Yes." I nodded and smiled.

"That's okay, then."

Yes, it was okay. It no longer bothered me to be called Um Ibrahim. In fact, I finally saw it as the mark of respect Muhammad had tried to tell me it was years ago. It no longer bothered me if some people thought birthing boys made me a better wife. I knew better, and so did everyone else I knew. Just as being called Mrs. Hallaj after marriage did not change who I was, neither did being called Um Ibrahim. It was a cultural difference and should be respected as such.

* * *

Shortly after Mazin's first birthday, Muhammad came home from work and found me in the kitchen. "I had lunch with Hanna Nasser today," he said.

"That's nice. Who is Hanna Nasser?" I was listening while preparing supper, my attention split between what he was saying and what I was doing.

"He's the president of Birzeit University near Ramallah, on the West Bank. He lives here now because he was expelled by the Occupation Forces."

"Why?"

When he got through laughing, he said, "They don't need a reason. They're the Occupying Power."

"Oh."

"Birzeit just became a four-year university and is in need of suitable faculty members. I accepted a job."

My head snapped up, and I dropped the knife I'd been

wielding. "The West Bank? The other side of the Jordan River? Palestine? In the Occupied Territories?"

"Yes. They need good people."

The phrase that came to mind was, going from the frying pan into the fire.

Appendix 1

From Ottoman Empire

to USA

THREE GENERATIONS OF HALLAJS

To say that there are enough books written about the history of Palestine to fill a library would be an understatement—and that is only considering the ones written in English. Each and every one of those books is different, many are contradictory, and they all have biases, conscious or not, based on the incomplete knowledge and the values and beliefs of the author. My history will be no different, but it is my intent to share my own limited knowledge in a short, pertinent, and intensely personal history.

* * *

Situated at the eastern shore of the Mediterranean Sea, Palestine sits at the busy crossroads connecting Europe, Asia, and Africa, a crossroads that saw a lot of traffic in the ages before air travel. Some heavy players who left their footprints include Ancient Egypt, Persia, Alexander the Great, the Roman Empire, the Byzantine Empire, several Muslim dynasties, and the Crusaders. On the heels of the Crusaders came the Ottoman Empire, whose rule lasted 400 years, ending at the very edge of living memory with its defeat in World War I.

Each of these great powers came to Palestine and the

surrounding region to keep the crossroads clear for their own purposes. They were, to borrow the words of Shakespeare, "a poor player that struts and frets his hour upon the stage and then is heard no more." This does not mean they did no harm, or that they did not oppress the people they ruled—some more than others.

The Ottoman rule is still remembered. More than one person told me that the Ottomans were responsible for denuding the hills of trees resulting in loss of soil and lack of the vegetation and root systems that keep moisture from evaporating and being lost before it can replenish either the soil or the water table. Reforestation is an ongoing process today.

The Ottoman Empire was desperate for soldiers near the end of World War I. The army sent detachments who rode through swaths of territory conscripting every able-bodied man and boy in the area, leaving only the old, infirm, or very young. This was devastating for small villages of subsistence farmers. Muhammad's grandfather was among those taken. He left a wife, Aisheh, and two young children, a boy named Yusef and a girl named Zerifeh. In his parting instructions, he repeatedly told his wife to educate Yusef.

* * *

Palestinians fought with the Allies in World War I to gain independence and rid themselves of the Ottoman rule. But before Yusef was old enough to go to school, the Ottomans had lost the war and the victors had divided the spoils. Palestine was placed under British Mandate. One of the core components of the Mandate was a document signed a year before the end of war—this simple letter from the Foreign Secretary of the United Kingdom to Lord Rothschild, a leader of the British Jewish community, called the Balfour Declaration.

This Declaration made the Israelis very different from the invaders of the past. They did not want merely to rule the land, they wanted to possess the land itself. They wanted the land without the people who had lived and farmed there for generations.

Foreign Office,

November 2nd, 1917.

Dear Lord Rothschild,

I have much pleasure in conveying to you, on behalf of His Majesty's Government, the following declaration of sympathy with Jewish Zionist aspirations which has been submitted to, and approved by, the Cabinet

His Majesty's Government view with favour the establishment in Palestine of a national home for the Jewish people, and will use their best endeavours to facilitate the achievement of this object, it being clearly understood that nothing shall be done which may prejudice the civil and religious rights of existing non-Jewish communities in Palestine, or the rights and political status enjoyed by Jews in any other country"

I should be grateful if you would bring this declaration to the knowledge of the Zionist Federation.

Public Domain photo taken from Wikipedia.org

Muhammad's grandmother neither knew nor cared. She could never have imagined that this single piece of paper would lead to what is often described as the world's most intractable conflict and pose an existential threat to her and the world as she knew it. Unaware, she set about fulfilling the promise to her long-gone husband. She sent Yusef to school. He was a stellar student and four years later "graduated" from the fourth grade with flying colors. The following year she took him back to school.

"My husband made me promise to educate Yusef. Four years is not an education." The head of the school explained that the school only went to fourth grade. "Four years is not enough. Make him start over and do another four years."

Four years had long been viewed as the measure of literacy. After four years, a student knew all that was needed to read, write, and do the arithmetic needed for daily life. Yusef now had enough education to be a clerk, which was as high as a native boy was expected to go. Not only was schooling limited to four years, it was further limited to boys. Muhammad's grandmother had never been to school and had little understanding of the mysteries of books, but she knew her son was not yet educated. A woman alone, raising two children on a bit of land, did not have the means to send her son to a boarding school in another town.

Meanwhile, instead of the independence they sought, the Palestinians found themselves the unwilling hosts of an influx of Zionist Jews who came from Europe and elsewhere as settlers, sponsored by England and the United States.

Zerifeh, Yusef's sister became a woman and married a distant cousin. Her first son was named Khalil, making her Amti Um Khalil. Her wedding lives only in my imagination, but her wedding dress lives in my closet.

The first summer we visited, she took me by the hand and led me to her bedroom. She opened her wardrobe and brought out a newspaper-wrapped package. Inside was the dress. Made of heavy silk, with each stitch lovingly placed by hand, it was a work of art. She told me to put it on, and we came out for a photo shoot on the veranda. When I took off the dress to return it, she told me to keep it. I said no.

I finally got Muhammad involved since my Arabic was not up to the task. "Tell her this is a family treasure, and it belongs with her descendants."

"She says she wants you to have it. She says, 'They will only scrub the floor with it when I die.' She knows you appreciate it."

I am still honored that a woman with a daughter and six sons would give me such a wonderful gift.

Amti Um Khalil's wedding dress circa 1920.

* * *

Muhammad's father, Yousef Saleh Hallaj, in his British police uniform.

Yusef joined the police force as a civil servant of Britain. He was tall and proud in his uniform. He, too, married and had three children: Saleh, Zahara, and Muhammad. His wife

186

died in childbirth when Muhammad was four years old. After a time Yusef married his deceased wife's half-sister, Fatima, reasoning that an aunt already had a connection with the children and would love them and raise them as her own.

* * *

As the British Mandate came to a close, the Palestinians were powerless to prevent the partition of their small country, about the size of Massachusetts, into two even smaller parts. In 1948 the British Mandate ended, and Palestinians watched, shocked and unbelieving, as their country disappeared beneath their feet. The United Nations established the state of Israel.

According to the plan, Israel was supposed to comprise 47% of the total, but the transition was far from peaceful. Well trained and well armed paramilitary groups carried out a series of attacks designed to terrorize and force the Palestinians from their homes even before the British forces had vacated the country. The British had effectively disarmed the Arab population during the Mandate, and any budding leaders had been either killed or exiled.

Before the dust settled, about 530 villages and cities had been destroyed, and about 15,000 Palestinians were killed. Qalqilya became a border city but remained on the Jordanian side of the new demarcation line. Luckily, none of our immediate family was among the casualties, although the citrus groves that had been their means of support were on the other side of the new lines.

When the dust finally did settle, 80% of the country lived under the Israeli flag. The remaining territory became part of Jordan, then named the Hashemite Kingdom of Transjordan. And so it was that Muhammad's grandmother, her children and grandchildren, were among the hundreds of thousands of Palestinians who became citizens of Jordan.

187

PHOTO: Blatant World via Flickr.com

An estimated 750,000 Palestinians from a population of 1.9 million people fled the violence and were "temporarily" housed in refugee camps, many in neighboring countries and even more in the West Bank, the part of Palestine that had become part of Jordan.

Saleh, already a husband and father, was called to serve in the army, but Muhammad was still a high school student. Upon graduation, he, too, was called to serve. Saleh found the military to his liking and remained in the army. Muhammad served the required number of years and decided to come to the United States to get a college degree.

* * *

The Six Day War in 1967 resulted in the capture of the remaining Palestinian territory by Israel. The West Bank and Gaza were governed by the Israeli military. One of the first things they did was take a census of all "non-Jewish inhabitants" of the area and issue identity cards. Anyone who was not physically present, which included people studying or working in other countries, did not get an identity card and was not allowed to return without special

188

permission.

Yusef, son of Grandmother Aisheh, lost the house he had lived in all his life, he lost the small plot of land his mother had cultivated to keep him fed, he lost the right to visit the land he had helped police for so many years, and he lost his right to pray in Al Aqsa Mosque in Jerusalem or to visit his first wife's grave. All because he had walked for days to reach Jordan and do his best to care for the family of his eldest son. He was not there for the census.

Muhammad lost the right to go home. He lost his right to show his children where he had been born and where he grew up. He lost his right to visit his aunts and cousins who lived in and around Qalqilya.

* * *

The Palestine Liberation Organization had been founded in 1964 with the goal of gathering support within the Arab states to pressure the international community to force Israel to withdraw from land taken by force.

After the 1967 war, a segment of the PLO became more militant and launched attacks on Israel from bases in Jordan. This caused problems along the border between Israel and Jordan a border that had been quiet and non-threatening. The King of Jordan was not happy.

In March 1968, Israel launched an attack on Karameh in reprisal for the raids, assuming the Jordanian army would ignore the incursion. Instead, the Jordanians provided artillery fire supporting the PLO guerilla fighters (fedayeen). For the first time the Israelis were forced to retreat. This was a huge moral victory that cemented the PLO national claims.

The PLO fighters moved into the towns and refugee camps in Jordan and began to provide services to the refugees. They set up clinics for basic health care, they often helped individual families in need. They helped set up cottage industries and organized youth activities. They began to blur the lines of sovereignty and issued travel documents that were accepted by many countries, allowing the bearers to go to the Gulf States and get more lucrative jobs than they could get in Jordan. The popularity of the PLO skyrocketed.

King Hussein saw the armed and well-organized movement as a threat—a "foreign" army within his borders. Their continued raids brought continued threats of retaliation from Israel. He told them to disarm, an order they could not obey and maintain their stated objectives. Negotiations were useless, and by September 1970 it erupted into open armed conflict—Black September.

———————————

https://www.youtube.com/watch?v=H7FML0wzJ6A -
Episode 1
The secret and not-so-secret events over the hundred years before the fall of the Ottoman Empire that led to the massive Jewish immigration in post-World War I Mandate period.

https://www.youtube.com/watch?v=yI2D5Fsd9lg -
Episode 2
Palestinian requests to limit immigration during British Mandate were refused and protests brutally suppressed. Arab nationalism was a capital crime while Jewish militia groups were armed and trained by the British.

https://www.youtube.com/watch?v=5SKECszemmA -
Episode 3
After 30 years, the British find the situation untenable and hand the problem to the United Nations. Partition was proposed, which started immediate expansion and actions to remove the Palestinians. In May 1948, Israel was created.

https://www.youtube.com/watch?v=0m_A7MlDrk -
Episode 4

By December 700,000 refugees were registered. West Bank and Gaza were made part of Jordan, and Palestine was erased from the maps. Today, more than 70 years later, the land confiscation and brutal repression of the Palestinians living under Israeli control continues.

Appendix 2
Map of Palestine

PALESTINIAN LOSS OF LAND 1946-2010

The first map shows Jewish *ownership* of land in Palestine at the time of the UN partition. The other three maps show Israeli *control* of land. Currently all of historical Palestine is under Israeli control.

_____

An interactive map:
https://interactive.aljazeera.com/aje/palestineremix/maps_main.html

192

Appendix 3
Saleh's House

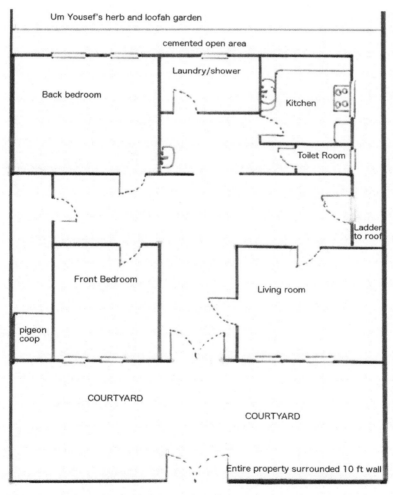

Um Yousef's herb and loofah garden

cemented open area

Laundry/shower

Back bedroom

Kitchen

Toilet Room

Ladder to roof

Front Bedroom

Living room

pigeon coop

COURTYARD

COURTYARD

Entire property surrounded 10 ft wall

Sidewalk and STREET

About the Author

DIXIANE HALLAJ spent eleven years in the Middle East as part of her husband's extended family, listening as they shared much of the refugee experience with her. In 2004, she visited refugee camps in Occupied Palestine, where she listened to the stories of many of the women. These stories formed the basis of her award-winning doctoral dissertation "Caught by Culture and Conflict" and her first two novels, *Born a Refugee* and *Checkpoint Kalandia*.

Find out more about Dixiane and her books on her social media and website.

Dixiane Hallaj Author on Facebook
@dixianehallaj on twitter and Instagram
Dixianehallaj.com
Sandhbooks.com

Acknowledgements

This book would never have been completed without the encouragement and suggestions of my writer friends and my aspiring writer friends. Special thanks go to Lenora Rain-Lee Good and Terry Korth Fischer who opened their hearts and their phone lines any time, night or day, when I needed them.

Made in the USA
Monee, IL
18 February 2021